New Haven Free
Public Library
133 Elm St.
New Haven, CT
06510

POETRY ROCKS!

Modern British Poetry

"The World Is Never the Same"

Enslow Publishers, Inc.
40 Industrial Road
Box 398
Berkeley Heights, NJ 07922
USA

http://www.enslow.com

"The world is never the same once a good poem has been added to it."
—Dylan Thomas

Copyright © 2010 by Michelle M. Houle

All rights reserved.

No part of this book may be reproduced by any means
without the written permission of the publisher.

Library of Congress Cataloging-in-Publication Data

Houle, Michelle M.
    Modern British poetry, "the world is never the same" / Michelle M. Houle.
       p. cm. — (Poetry rocks!)
    Includes bibliographical references and index.
    ISBN-13: 978-0-7660-3278-1
    ISBN-10: 0-7660-3278-7
    1. English poetry—History and criticism—Juvenile literature. 2. Poets, English—
Biography—Juvenile literature. I. Title.
    PR502.H66 2010
    821'.809—dc22
                                          2009015880

Paperback ISBN 978-1-59845-381-2

Printed in the United States of America
042011 Lake Book Manufacturing, Inc., Melrose Park, IL

10 9 8 7 6 5 4 3 2

To Our Readers: We have done our best to make sure all Internet addresses in this book were active and appropriate when we went to press. However, the author and the publisher have no control over and assume no liability for the material available on those Internet sites or on other Web sites they may link to. Any comments or suggestions can be sent by e-mail to comments@enslow.com or to the address on the back cover. We have made every effort to locate all copyright holders of material used in this book. If any omissions or errors have occurred, corrections will be made in future editions.

♻ Enslow Publishers, Inc., is committed to printing our books on recycled paper. The paper in every book contains 10% to 30% post-consumer waste (PCW). The cover board on the outside of each book contains 100% PCW. Our goal is to do our part to help young people and the environment too!

Illlustration Credits: Associated Press, p. 134; Clipart.com, pp. 12 (lower right), 63; Everett Collection, pp. 86, 120, 129, 141; Getty Images, pp. 98, 110, 115; Library of Congress, pp. 12 (upper left, upper right, lower left), 75; National Archives and Records Administration, p. 105; Photos. com, pp. 9, 18, 26, 38, 51; Shutterstock, pp. 1, 5, 16, 25, 37, 50, 57, 62, 74, 84, 97, 109, 119, 133; Wikimedia Commons, p. 69.

Cover Illustration: Shutterstock.

Contents

Permissions

"Still Falls the Rain," "Aubade," and "Sir Beelzebub" (from Façade), from THE COLLECTED POEMS OF EDITH SITWELL by Edith Sitwell, originally published by the Vanguard Press, Inc. Copyright © 1968 by The Vanguard Press. Copyright 1949, 1953, 1954, © 1959, 1962, 1963 by Dame Edith Sitwell. Reprinted by permission of Harold Ober Associates, Inc.

"Musée des Beaux Arts," copyright 1940 & renewed 1968 by W. H. Auden, "The Unknown Citizen," copyright 1940 & renewed 1968 by W. H. Auden, and "In Memory of W. B. Yeats" by copyright 1940 & renewed 1968 by W. H. Auden, from COLLECTED POEMS by W. H. Auden. Used by permission of Random House, Inc.

"Not Waving But Drowning" and "Tender Only to One" by Stevie Smith, from THE COL-LECTED POEMS OF STEVIE SMITH, copyright © 1972 by Stevie Smith. Reprinted by permission of New Directions Publishing Corp.

"Do Not Go Gentle Into That Good Night" by Dylan Thomas, from THE POEMS OF DYLAN THOMAS, copyright © 1952 by Dylan Thomas. Reprinted by permission of New Directions Publishing Corp.

"Fern Hill" by Dylan Thomas, from THE POEMS OF DYLAN THOMAS, copyright © 1945 by The Trustees for the Copyrights of Dylan Thomas. Reprinted by permission of New Directions Publishing Corp.

"The Force That Through the Green Fuse Drives the Flower" by Dylan Thomas, from THE POEMS OF DYLAN THOMAS, copyright © 1939 New Directions Publishing Corp. Re-printed by permission of New Directions Publishing Corp.

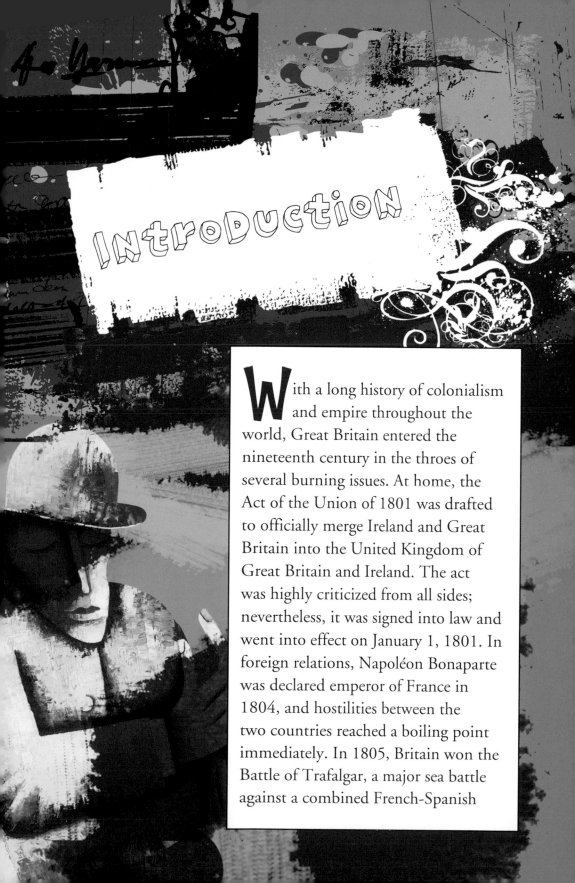

INTRODUCTION

With a long history of colonialism and empire throughout the world, Great Britain entered the nineteenth century in the throes of several burning issues. At home, the Act of the Union of 1801 was drafted to officially merge Ireland and Great Britain into the United Kingdom of Great Britain and Ireland. The act was highly criticized from all sides; nevertheless, it was signed into law and went into effect on January 1, 1801. In foreign relations, Napoléon Bonaparte was declared emperor of France in 1804, and hostilities between the two countries reached a boiling point immediately. In 1805, Britain won the Battle of Trafalgar, a major sea battle against a combined French-Spanish fleet. As the decade progressed, Napoléon turned his attention to other parts of Europe, especially Russia, which he attacked in 1812. His actions were closely watched as the growing French Empire continued to threaten the stability of the United Kingdom.

While these political challenges were fought in the courtroom and the battlefield, changes in manufacturing, agriculture, and transportation were leading the country toward the Industrial Revolution, as it is known today. While this was considered progress by some, it was also a major shock to society. As Napoléon was marching toward Russia, linen workers rioted and attacked factories, smashing the machinery that they feared would soon replace them.

In the midst of all this conflict, the United States declared war on Britain on June 1, 1812, because, in part, of Britain's practice

FACTS

Rhyme Schemes

A rhyme scheme is a pattern of rhyming words within a poem. Rhyme schemes are identified by assigning a letter of the alphabet to each sound at the end of a line. For example, in the last stanza of the Auden poem "In Memory of W. B. Yeats," lines one and two ("heart" and "start") rhyme, so they are assigned the letter a. The next two lines end with "days" and "praise." They are assigned the letter b because they are different from a but similar to each other:

In the deserts of the heart (a)
Let the healing fountain start, (a)
In the prison of his days (b)
Teach the free man how to praise. (b)

Thus, the complete rhyme scheme is aabb.[1]

of impressing, or forcing, sailors into their navy. The war with the
United States continued through the end of 1814, although a treaty
was not ratified until 1815. Soon after the treaty was signed with the
United States, a final battle was fought between Britain and France,
the Battle of Waterloo. At this battle, Napoléon was finally defeated
for the last time. He died in exile in 1821 on the island of St. Helena
in the Atlantic Ocean.

Despite all this chaos, the early nineteenth century was also
a time of positive growth in the arts, especially in literature.
Following on the heels of the French Revolution, writers in the
United Kingdom began to emulate their French counterparts
with a new style of writing known as romanticism. Developed in
reaction to industrialization and the eighteenth century's "Age of
Enlightenment," this movement emphasized emotion, nature, the
experience of common people, and the development of a national
folklore. Major early romantic writers include Lord Byron, Samuel
Coleridge, John Keats, Percy Bysshe Shelley, Mary Wollstonecraft
Shelley, and William Wordsworth. They will not be covered in this
volume, which deals with poets born after 1800.

During this time, the novel was continuing to rise in esteem as
a literary art form. In the early years of the nineteenth century, for
example, Jane Austen commented on social issues and the lives of the
gentry through novels like *Pride and Prejudice* and *Emma*. Through
her novel *Northanger Abbey*, Austen took aim at the popularity of
the gothic novel, which combined traits of both horror stories with
romances and which had held sway over the public in the latter
quarter of the eighteenth century. Walter Scott's novel *Waverley*, on
the other hand, was considered one of the first historical novels upon
its publication in 1814, and it was hugely popular throughout the
world.

Queen Victoria

In 1837, William IV was succeeded to the throne by his niece Victoria. Queen Victoria's reign, which continued until her death in 1901, is often noted as the height of the British Empire and Britain's Industrial Revolution. Major social developments during her reign included child labor laws, an increase in women's rights, and educational reform. It was also an era of great creative activity in Britain, and much of the writing of the period dealt with issues of the times such as industrialization, the rapid growth of cities, science, and societal issues. Some of the most noted British novelists of this time included the Brontë sisters, George Eliot, Charles Dickens, Thomas Hardy, Lewis Carroll, and Robert Louis Stevenson. Hardy was also a poet who wrote prolifically into the early twentieth century. The visual arts were dominated in part by the Pre-Raphaelite Brotherhood, a group of artists that included William Holman Hunt, Sir John Everett Millais, Dante Gabriel Rossetti, and William Michael Rossetti. They wanted to reform art by returning to what they saw as simplicity and truthfulness of art before Raphael, an influential Renaissance painter. In 1859, Charles Darwin published his famous book *On the Origin of Species,* in which he detailed his theories on natural selection.

In celebration of modern industry and design, the first World's Fair was held in 1851 at the Crystal Palace, a huge glass and iron structure built for the fair, which was called the Great Exhibition. One of the main outcomes of the exhibition was an interest in photography, which was a burgeoning art form at the time.

The world, at this time, was also becoming more and more connected. In 1838, regular Atlantic steamship service began, making it easier to travel back and forth to the Americas. In 1840, the Royal Mail instituted the "penny post," which allowed letter writers to buy

Queen Victoria reigned from 1837 to 1901, and gave her name to one of the most illustrious eras in British history.

prepaid adhesive stamps for mail sent within the United Kingdom. The first telegraph cable was laid under the Atlantic in 1866, and the Suez Canal opened in 1869.

Early Twentieth Century

Queen Victoria died in 1901 at the age of eighty-one. She was succeeded by King Edward VII, whose reign corresponded with Britain's "Belle Epoque," or beautiful era, so named because it was a period of calm with great developments in the arts. Novelists such as Joseph Conrad, E. M. Forster, and H. G. Wells wrote prolifically during this decade, and plays by George Bernard Shaw and the Norwegian Henrik Ibsen were very popular. Live, outdoor musical performances, especially by brass bands, were common.

On June 28, 1914, the calm ended when the Archduke Franz Ferdinand of Austria, the heir to the Austro-Hungarian throne, was assassinated in Sarajevo. This event would spark conflict across Europe as an intricate series of alliances threw the continent into war. Britain entered the fray almost immediately when it declared war on Germany in August 1914 after Germany invaded Belgium. In April 1917, the United States joined the war on the side of the British and its allies, which included France, Russia, and Italy, and their associated colonies. After fierce fighting, Germany signed a truce agreement, or armistice, with Britain in November 1918, and the 1919 Treaty of Versailles virtually redrew the map of Europe and other key parts of the world.

The 1920s saw a period of artistic rebirth, highlighted by the establishment of artist communities in Paris and, to some extent, in Germany. During this time, the modernist movement–which was marked by deliberate breaks from and experiments in traditional subject and form–was at its height. Some of the movement's famous novelists include James Joyce, Virginia Woolf, Ernest Hemingway, and D. H. Lawrence, who was also a prolific poet. Modern American poets included Ezra Pound, T. S. Eliot, H. D., Marianne Moore, William Carlos Williams, and Gertrude Stein. Modernist artists include Pablo Picasso and Henri Matisse, who were both friends and rivals. Igor Stravinsky and Arnold Schoenberg were noted

FACTS

Poetic Meter

The meter in a poem is measured by the number of stressed syllables in a line. Each unit of syllables within a line is called a foot, which has one stressed syllable (marked with a /) and three, two, one, or no unstressed syllables (marked with a ∪). Lines lengths are labeled as follows:

> one foot: monometer
> two feet: dimeter
> three feet: trimeter
> four feet: tetrameter
> five feet: pentameter.

Lines of six or seven feet (hexameter or heptameter) are seen in other languages such as French or Greek, but do not sound harmonious in English.

There are several common patterns for a metrical foot:

> iambic (∪ /) ("When in disgrace with fortune and men's eyes")
> trochaic (/ ∪) ("Mary had a little lamb")
> dactylic (/ ∪ ∪) ("Listen, my children, and you shall hear")
> anapestic (∪ ∪ /) ("'Twas the night before Christmas")
> spondee (/ /) ("hot dog")[2]

Among the best-known modernist American poets were (clockwise from upper left) Marianne Moore, T. S. Eliot, Ezra Pound, and William Carlos Williams.

as major modernist composers because of their experiments with atonality and other breaks from musical convention. In 1922, further cultural and scientific advances were seen with the formation of the British Broadcasting Corporation, or BBC, which broadcast plays, concerts, and other programs over the radio. In 1927, the advent of the "talkies," or motion pictures with sound, had a great impact on artistic and popular culture.

The March Toward War

During the 1930s, the United States and Europe fell into the Great Depression. Over the next few years, Adolf Hitler and Benito Mussolini rose to power in Germany and Italy, aided in part by the social and economic problems in their countries. By the late 1930s, war was on the horizon. In March 1938, Austria was taken over by Germany, which was under the rule of Hitler and the Nazis. Germany continued its territorial expansion, and Britain declared war in September 1939 after Germany invaded Poland. In the spring of the following year, Winston Churchill became the prime minister. In the summer of 1940, Germany began its attacks on Britain. It occupied several outlying islands in the English Channel, and in August 1940, it began to regularly bomb the mainland through a series of air raids known as the Blitz, or "blitzkrieg," which means "lightning war." The worst bombings were in London, though the German air force also attacked other cities, including Liverpool in the north of England and Belfast in Northern Ireland.

In the fall of 1940, the Axis powers were officially established when Germany, Italy, and Japan signed the Tripartite Pact. The international conflict grew, and by the end of 1941, the United States had also entered into war after Japan bombed Pearl Harbor on December 7. At first, the war went poorly for the Allies, which

Elizabeth Barrett Browning
(1806–1861)

Elizabeth Barrett was born on March 6, 1806, the eldest of twelve children. Her father was the heir to a Jamaican plantation fortune, and her mother was from a well-to-do family. Although it appears that she was healthy in her early childhood, Elizabeth suffered some kind of lung complaint in her teens, and she was then considered to be frail for the rest of her life. Sometime in her teens, she also began taking opium for pain, possibly following a spinal injury. Doctors commonly prescribed opium at the time, and this was a habit Elizabeth would have for the rest of her life.[1]

Elizabeth was an intelligent, precocious child. At the age of twelve, she wrote an epic poem entitled "The Battle of Marathon," which her parents printed privately and distributed with pride. Elizabeth continued to write through her late teens. Her first collection of poems, *An Essay on Mind and Other Poems,* was published anonymously in 1826 when she was twenty.

Tragedy struck the household when Elizabeth's mother passed away in 1828 when Elizabeth was twenty-two. Her father's fortunes then took a turn for the worse, and the family was forced to move to London. Despite these challenges, Barrett continued to write, and her next collection of poems, *The Seraphim and Other Poems,* was published in 1838 under her name. The collection received very positive notices, and Barrett was quickly recognized as an accomplished poet. She began to correspond with such important literary figures as Thomas Carlyle, Edgar Allan Poe, and William Wordsworth.

After *The Seraphim* was published, Barrett became ill again. Because she suffered from lung problems, her doctor recommended that she go to Torquay, where it was warmer. In 1838, she went there with three of her siblings, including her brother Edward, whom she affectionately called "Bro." In July 1840, Bro was killed in a boating accident near Torquay. According to Sarah K. Bolton, in her 1886 book *The Lives of Girls Who Became Famous,* Bro's death nearly destroyed Barrett: "She blamed herself for his death, because he came to Torquay for her comfort. All winter long she heard the sound of waves ringing in her ears like the moans of the dying."[2]

After a nervous breakdown, Barrett returned to her father's house in London in the fall of 1841. For the next several years, she did not leave the house and she accepted only a few visitors. In 1844, her collection *Poems* was published, again to great acclaim. It was this book that brought Barrett to the attention of Robert Browning when he was given the book by John Kenyon, Browning's friend and Barrett's cousin. After reading the volume, Browning wrote to Barrett, who received the letter happily—she had read some of Browning's work and had been so impressed that she had referenced him in one of the pieces in *Poems*. As she wrote to another friend, "I had a letter from Browning the poet last night ... which threw me into ecstasies!"[3]

The pair began to correspond frequently, sometimes as often as three times a day. They met for the first time in May 1845, and

Elizabeth Barrett Browning

though they saw each other only occasionally after that, their love blossomed through their letters. Their correspondence was kept a secret for the most part because of Barrett's father, who refused to allow his children to marry. It was not until the fall of 1846—when she was forty years old—that Barrett decided to break from her father and marry Browning. After a private ceremony, the Brownings left England for Italy, where they lived for the rest of her life. In 1849, Barrett Browning gave birth to a son, Robert Weidemann Barrett Browning, who was known as Pen. Despite repeated efforts by the Brownings, and even after the birth of Pen, Edward Barrett refused to forgive his daughter, and he never spoke to her again. He died in 1857.

Barrett Browning's success as a poet was well recognized during her lifetime. In 1850, she was a lead candidate to succeed Wordsworth as England's poet laureate, although Tennyson ultimately received the honor. Some of her best-known poems were published in the last decade of her life, including *Sonnets from the Portuguese* (1850), which include her early love poems to Robert Browning; *Casa Guidi Windows* (1851), which takes its title from the Brownings' home in Florence, and in which she expresses her sympathy for the Italian struggle for unification; and *Aurora Leigh* (1857), possibly her most famous and mature work which, in part, tells the story of a woman's independence from a domineering man.

On the night of June 29, 1861, Barrett Browning died in her husband's arms. She was buried in the English cemetery in Florence. The popularity of Barrett Browning's work declined in the early twentieth century. Despite attempts by such notable authors as Virginia Woolf, it was only in the late twentieth century that serious interest in her work was revived.

Sonnet 13

And wilt thou have me fashion into speech
The love I bear thee, finding words enough,
And hold the torch out, while the winds are rough,
Between our faces, to cast light on each?—
I drop it at thy feet. I cannot teach
My hand to hold my spirit so far off
From myself—me—that I should bring thee proof
In words, of love hid in me out of reach.
Nay, let the silence of my womanhood
Commend my woman-love to thy belief,—
Seeing that I stand unwon, however wooed,
And rend the garment of my life, in brief,
By a most dauntless, voiceless fortitude,
Lest one touch of this heart convey its grief.

wooed—courted, sought the love of

rend—to rip or tear

dauntless—fearless

Summary and Explication: "Sonnet 13"

After her marriage, Elizabeth Barrett Browning published *Sonnets from the Portuguese,* forty-four poems dedicated to Browning. The "Portuguese" in the title refers to herself, since Browning thought Barrett Browning looked Portuguese because of her dark hair. The poems were mostly written during the couple's courtship.

In the first two lines of this poem, the speaker asks if it is necessary for her to put her love into words, a task that does not seem possible because her love is so strong. If it were possible to describe her love, she then asks if it would be necessary for her to present the words publicly as a "torch" that would then illuminate them both—or make their identities public. In doing so, the speaker suggests that the words—and their love—will be open to critique from society, as represented by the "rough winds." In lines five through eight, the speaker says that she cannot hold the "torch," which represents her love and which she drops at her love's feet: She claims she cannot put her love out so publicly, because it is hidden within her out of reach of words, unable to be proven. In lines nine through eleven, the speaker asks her love to take her silence as proof of her love. This silence is proper because of her "womanhood," since she is "unwon, however wooed"—or unmarried although courted. She then says that her love is so strong that she would rather tear her life apart than share any grief with her love.

Techniques and Devices

A sonnet is a fourteen-line poem that usually follows a specific rhyme scheme and meter. Here, the rhyme scheme is roughly that of a Petrarchan sonnet, with an octave (eight lines) of *abbaabba* rhyme and a sextet (six lines) of *cdcdcd.* A sonnet series was traditionally written by a man in honor of a woman whom he considered his muse. Similar series were written by such famous poets as Dante, Petrarch, and Shakespeare.

InterpreTaTion

In *Sonnets from the Portuguese,* Barrett Browning adopts the sonnet series structure—traditionally used by men—for her own purpose, and in doing so, takes the traditions of the series and complicates them. In Sonnet 13, Barrett Browning contends that, as a woman, she is not able to "fashion into speech," or put into words, her feelings. However, by pointing out the struggle in a poem—in words—she makes her love, and her ability to convey this love, clear.

Discussion Questions

1. In this poem, does it seem as if Barrett Browning has simply reversed the gender roles typical of poet to a beloved in a sonnet series? Why or why not?

2. What language suggests that the speaker respects the talent of the beloved in this poem?

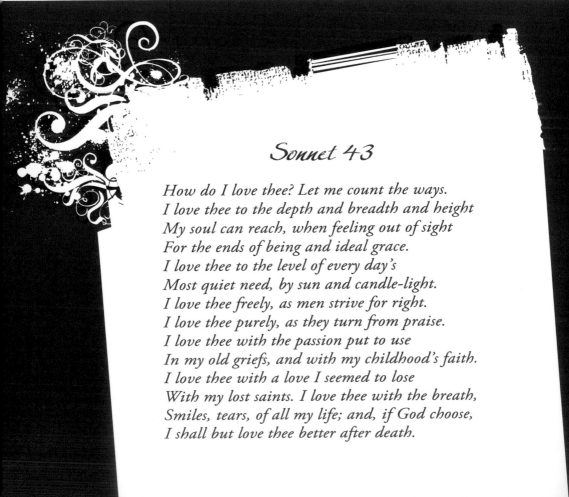

Sonnet 43

How do I love thee? Let me count the ways.
I love thee to the depth and breadth and height
My soul can reach, when feeling out of sight
For the ends of being and ideal grace.
I love thee to the level of every day's
Most quiet need, by sun and candle-light.
I love thee freely, as men strive for right.
I love thee purely, as they turn from praise.
I love thee with the passion put to use
In my old griefs, and with my childhood's faith.
I love thee with a love I seemed to lose
With my lost saints. I love thee with the breath,
Smiles, tears, of all my life; and, if God choose,
I shall but love thee better after death.

Discussion Questions

1. To what extremes does the speaker love her beloved? What language shows this? What impact does this have on your reading of the poem?

2. Sonnet 43 is one of the most famous poems in the English language. Why do you think this poem is so memorable?

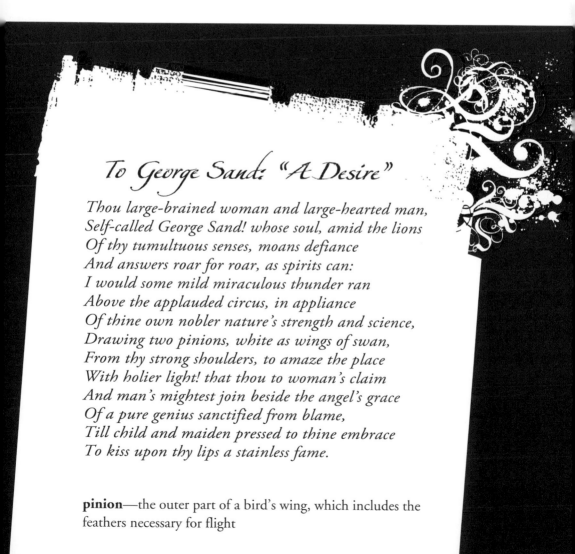

To George Sand: "A Desire"

Thou large-brained woman and large-hearted man,
Self-called George Sand! whose soul, amid the lions
Of thy tumultuous senses, moans defiance
And answers roar for roar, as spirits can:
I would some mild miraculous thunder ran
Above the applauded circus, in appliance
Of thine own nobler nature's strength and science,
Drawing two pinions, white as wings of swan,
From thy strong shoulders, to amaze the place
With holier light! that thou to woman's claim
And man's mightest join beside the angel's grace
Of a pure genius sanctified from blame,
Till child and maiden pressed to thine embrace
To kiss upon thy lips a stainless fame.

pinion—the outer part of a bird's wing, which includes the feathers necessary for flight

FACTS

George Sand

George Sand was the pseudonym of Amandine Aurore Lucile Dupin, a French novelist and feminist who defied convention by wearing men's clothes and smoking in public. Elizabeth Barrett Browning, like many of her contemporaries, greatly admired George Sand and her work. This poem, along with "To George Sand: A Recognition," was published in Barrett Browning's 1844 collection of poems. She ultimately met George Sand in 1852.

Discussion Questions

1. This poem suggests that George Sand complicates the notion that certain attributes are feminine and others masculine. What indicates this and why? What do you think of these divisions?

2. What image is used to describe Sand and why?

Read More

Browning, Elizabeth Barrett. *Sonnets from the Portuguese.* New York: Crown, 1980.

Stack, V. E., ed. *How Do I Love Thee? The Love-Letters of Robert Browning and Elizabeth Barrett.* New York: Putnam, 1969.

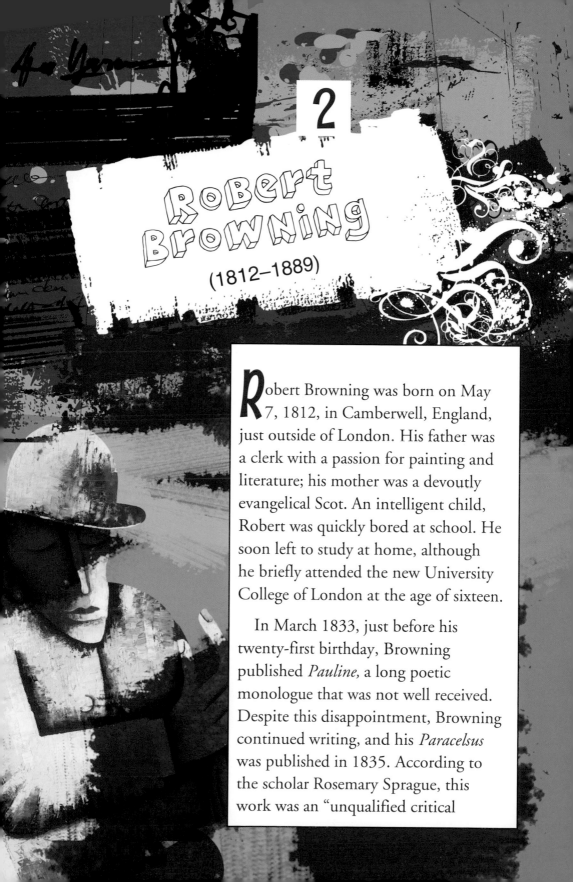

Robert Browning

(1812–1889)

Robert Browning was born on May 7, 1812, in Camberwell, England, just outside of London. His father was a clerk with a passion for painting and literature; his mother was a devoutly evangelical Scot. An intelligent child, Robert was quickly bored at school. He soon left to study at home, although he briefly attended the new University College of London at the age of sixteen.

In March 1833, just before his twenty-first birthday, Browning published *Pauline,* a long poetic monologue that was not well received. Despite this disappointment, Browning continued writing, and his *Paracelsus* was published in 1835. According to the scholar Rosemary Sprague, this work was an "unqualified critical

Robert Browning

success," which propelled Browning to literary stardom.[1] During this time, Browning began to travel throughout Europe, and he briefly served as a diplomatic secretary to St. Petersburg in Russia. In the late 1830s, Browning tried his hand at writing plays, and the interest in drama continued with his *Dramatic Lyrics,* which was published in 1842 and included the poem "My Last Duchess," among others.

In 1844, Browning read a volume of poetry by Elizabeth Barrett, who was widely praised as one of the most notable poets of the time. The volume included a poem entitled "Lady Geraldine's Courtship," in which Barrett referenced Browning among other notable poets, such as Wordsworth and Tennyson. Soon after reading the volume, Browning wrote to Barrett on January 10, 1845, and said, "I love your verses with all my heart, dear Miss Barrett ... and I love you too."[2] An invalid with a domineering father, Barrett did not allow Browning to visit her until May 1845, although they wrote letters constantly during that time. After their first meeting, they continued to write, and within a year, they were secretly engaged. Browning and Barrett were married in a private ceremony on September 12, 1846. Concerned about Elizabeth's father's reaction—he had forbidden his children to marry—the couple immediately left England for Italy. A few years later, they had a son, Robert Weidemann "Pen" Browning, who was born on March 9, 1849, in Florence, which was their main home for fifteen years. While living in Florence, both Brownings continued writing, though it was Elizabeth who garnered most of the praise. In 1855, Browning's *Men and Women* was published. Although today's scholars consider many of the pieces in *Men and Women* to be some of Browning's best poems, contemporary critics panned the work. For the next few years, Browning wrote little. Elizabeth soon became very ill, and she died in Florence on June 29, 1861.

Grief stricken, Browning returned to England with his son and eventually, he began to write again. In 1863, his *Dramatis Personae* was well received, which helped him to regain some of his stature as a poet. In 1868, Browning published *The Ring and the Book,* a long series of dramatic poems documenting the seventeenth-century murder of a young woman and the priest who tried to save her from a brutal husband. *The Ring and the Book* was immediately recognized as a masterpiece, and because of it, Browning's place in literature was assured. He rose in society, and soon received honorary degrees from Oxford, Cambridge, and the University of Edinburgh. In the later years of his life, he wrote prolifically, and he was considered a celebrity of high standing. He corresponded with such luminaries as Thomas Carlyle; Charles Dickens; Alfred, Lord Tennyson; Matthew Arnold; and many others. In 1881, the Robert Browning Society was founded by some of Browning's admirers in England and America. Today he is considered one of the most important Victorian poets.

In late 1889, Browning caught a cold after walking in Venice, where he was visiting his son, who had become a painter. The cold quickly worsened and Browning died on December 12, 1889, the same day his final book of poems, *Asolando,* was published. A funeral was held in Venice, and messages of sympathy from Queen Victoria and from King Victor Emanuel of Italy were read at the service.[3] Although Browning had wanted to be buried next to Elizabeth in the English cemetery in Florence, the cemetery was no longer accepting new burials.[4] Instead, Browning received one of England's highest honors, and he was buried in the famed Poets' Corner in Westminster Abbey in London.

My Last Duchess

That's my last Duchess painted on the wall,
Looking as if she were alive. I call
That piece a wonder, now: Frà Pandolf's hands
Worked busily a day, and there she stands.
Will 't please you sit and look at her? I said
'Frà Pandolf' by design, for never read
Strangers like you that pictured countenance,
The depth and passion of its earnest glance,
But to myself they turned (since none puts by
The curtain I have drawn for you, but I)
And seemed as they would ask me, if they durst,
How such a glance came there; so, not the first
Are you to turn and ask thus. Sir, 't was not
Her husband's presence only, called that spot
Of joy into the Duchess' cheek: perhaps
Frà Pandolf chanced to say, 'Her mantle laps
Over my lady's wrist too much,' or 'Paint
Must never hope to reproduce the faint
Half-flush that dies along her throat:' such stuff
Was courtesy, she thought, and cause enough
For calling up that spot of joy. She had
A heart—how shall I say?—too soon made glad,
Too easily impressed; she liked whate'er
She looked on, and her looks went everywhere.
Sir, 't was all one! My favour at her breast,
The dropping of the daylight in the West,
The bough of cherries some officious fool
Broke in the orchard for her, the white mule
She rode with round the terrace—all and each
Would draw from her alike the approving speech,
Or blush, at least. She thanked men, —good! but thanked

Somehow—I know not how—as if she ranked
My gift of a nine-hundred-years-old name
With anybody's gift. Who'd stoop to blame
This sort of trifling? Even had you skill

In speech—(which I have not)—to make your will
Quite clear to such an one, and say, 'Just this
Or that in you disgusts me; here you miss,
Or there exceed the mark'—and if she let
Herself be lessoned so, nor plainly set
Her wits to yours, forsooth, and made excuse,
E'en then would be some stooping; and I choose
Never to stoop. Oh, sir, she smiled, no doubt,
Whene'er I passed her; but who passed without
Much the same smile? This grew; I gave commands;
Then all smiles stopped together. There she stands
As if alive. Will 't please you rise? We'll meet
The company below then. I repeat,
The Count your master's known munificence
Is ample warrant that no just pretence
Of mine for dowry will be disallowed;
Though his fair daughter's self, as I avowed
At starting, is my object. Nay, we'll go
Together down, sir. Notice Neptune, though,
Taming a sea-horse, thought a rarity,
Which Claus of Innsbruck cast in bronze for me!

countenance—face

durst—dare

forsooth—indeed

munificence—generosity

disallowed—rejected as untrue or improper

Summary and Explication: "My Last Duchess"

This is one of Browning's most famous and often discussed poems, which was written in the form of a dramatic monologue. The speaker is a duke who may have been modeled after a historical figure, Alfonso II, the fifth Duke of Ferrara. Alfonso II was first married to Lucrezia de Medici, who was only fourteen when they married and who died under suspicious circumstances. Alfonso later married the daughter of the Count of Tyrol, whose capital was Innsbruck.[5] The artists referenced by the duke in the poem, Frà Pandolf and Claus of Innsbruck, were probably imagined by Browning.[6]

The duke is showing his art collection to a visitor who has come to arrange his next marriage. The poem opens with the duke inviting the visitor to look at a painting of his late wife, the previous duchess. The portrait was painted by Frà Pandolf, and the speaker suggests that this is a particularly special painting since no one gets to look at it without his permission (as indicated by the parenthetical "since none puts by / The curtain drawn for you, but I"). The duke then begins a digression about the painting—and the woman in it—seemingly in the response to a question posed to him by the visitor, though the reader hears no such question. The duke seems obsessed with what he sees as an overly passionate look, or "glance," on the face of his late wife. He then goes on to say it "was not / Her husband's presence only, called that spot / Of joy into the Duchess' cheek," or rather that the duchess would look passionately at men besides her husband. For example, the duke thought that his wife would blush at even the slightest courtesy spoken by the painter. He says, "She had / A heart—how shall I say?—too soon made glad," and he says that everything made her happy and passionate. For the duke, his late wife's main flaw was that she was equally moved by him and by the sunset, the cherries given to her by a peasant, and the mule she rode. In other words, she was indiscriminate in her affections—at least, according to the duke. His continued emphasis on this "flaw" indicates his obsession with it. For example, he points out that she "thanked men," which was proper, but he said she gave thanks for trivialities with the same enthusiasm as she did her marriage to the duke. Despite the fact that this enthusiasm infuriated the duke, he never said anything because that would be "stooping" to her, which he refused to do. Eventually, he gave the order to have her killed: "This grew; I gave commands; / Then all smiles stopped together." As soon as the duke shares this information with the visitor, he abruptly stops speaking about his late wife and turns to speaking about the proposed dowry for his future bride. The poem ends with the duke pointing out another artwork in his collection, a bronze statue of Neptune.

FACTS

Poets' Corner in Westminster Abbey

Westminster Abbey is a large gothic-style church in London. It is the traditional site for coronations and the burial of British monarchs. The Poets' Corner is in the southern part of the church, and a number of noted poets, playwrights, and writers are buried or commemorated there. Geoffrey Chaucer was the first person to be buried in Poets' Corner. Other writers buried there include Robert Browning, Charles Dickens, and Alfred, Lord Tennyson. Some of the writers who have been memorialized with plaques include Jane Austen, the Brontë sisters, Wilfred Owen, William Shakespeare, Dylan Thomas, and William Wordsworth.

Techniques and Devices

A dramatic monologue is a type of poem in which a person, who is *not* the poet, speaks the entire poem at a specific moment and to a specific person or people. The listeners within the poem do not speak or their words are not represented within the poem; only the speaker's reaction to the listeners is represented. The dramatic monologue serves to illustrate the speaker's character.

Interpretation

Throughout his monologue, the duke implies that he has trouble finding the right words to speak about his late wife—he says, "how shall I say?" and "I know not how"—but this is a performance, as is the act of showing the painting to the messenger who has come to arrange his next marriage ("none puts by / The curtain I have drawn for you, but I"). The duke had been angered by what he saw as his first wife's inability or unwillingness to discriminate, or judge. More than that, however, he viewed this as an act of treason, punishable by death, which he feels he has the power to order without judge or jury. The duke shows himself to be all too willing to judge—and condemn—her for this "trifling," and he makes this willingness very clear to the person responsible for arranging his next marriage. This illustrates his violent, vindictive, and dangerously powerful character.

Discussion Questions

1. How is the "last Duchess" like a trophy to the duke? What language suggests this and why?

2. What kind of message does the duke imply when he points out the bronze statue of Neptune "Taming a sea-horse"?

Meeting at Night

I.

The grey sea and the long black land;
And the yellow half-moon large and low;
And the startled little waves that leap
In fiery ringlets from their sleep,
As I gain the cove with pushing prow,
And quench its speed i' the slushy sand.

II.

Then a mile of warm sea-scented beach;
Three fields to cross till a farm appears;
A tap at the pane, the quick sharp scratch
And blue spurt of a lighted match,
And a voice less loud, through its joys and fears,
Than the two hearts beating each to each!

cove—a sheltered area on a shore

prow—the front part of a boat or the boat itself

Discussion Questions

1. This poem was originally published in 1845 in *Dramatic Romances and Lyrics*. It was originally two poems entitled "Night" and "Morning" and was combined as above in 1849. How do these two stanzas seem to distinguish nighttime in contrast to morning?

2. What is the rhyme scheme of this poem?

Home-Thoughts, from Abroad

I

Oh, to be in England
Now that April's there,
And whoever wakes in England
Sees, some morning, unaware,
That the lowest boughs and the brushwood sheaf
Round the elm-tree bole are in tiny leaf,
While the chaffinch sings on the orchard bough
In England—now!

II.

And after April, when May follows,
And the whitethroat builds, and all the swallows!
Hark, where my blossomed pear-tree in the hedge
Leans to the field and scatters on the clover
Blossoms and dewdrops—at the bent spray's edge—
That's the wise thrush; he sings each song twice over,
Lest you should think he never could recapture
The first fine careless rapture!
And through the fields look rough with hoary dew,
All will be gay when noontide wakes anew
The buttercups, the little children's dower
Far brighter than this gaudy melon-flower!

chaffinch—a small, common songbird

Discussion Questions

1. This poem was originally published as part of a larger poem that included "Here's to Nelson's Memory" and "Home-Thoughts, from the Sea," although the original manuscript suggests that they were not originally thought of as companion pieces.[7] The poems are often seen as illustrating a traveler's enthusiasm for the British Empire, which experienced significant growth during the reign of Queen Victoria. How does Browning's speaker idealize home here, and why do you think he or she feels this way?

2. The speaker here is drawn to the details of a rural scene—but one that has no people in it. What is the impact of these minute details? What does the absence of people suggest about the traveler's homesickness?

Read More

Garret, Martin. *Elizabeth Barrett Browning and Robert Browning.* New York: Oxford University Press, 2001.

Gillooly, Eileen, ed. *Robert Browning.* New York: Sterling, 2000.

3

ALFRED, LORD TENNYSON

(1809–1892)

Alfred Tennyson was born on August 6, 1809, in Somersby, England, the fourth of twelve children. Alfred's grandfather had been a wealthy businessman who had risen to claim a seat in Parliament. Alfred's father became a clergyman, and though the family was relatively well-to-do, they never achieved the status of some of their wealthy relatives. After a few years in Louth grammar school—which he apparently hated—Alfred was withdrawn from school to study with his father at home. As a youngster, Alfred read the work of Alexander Pope, Sir Walter Scott, Lord Byron, and Percy Bysshe Shelley, and he began writing poetry at a young age.

Alfred, Lord Tennyson

In 1827, Alfred entered Trinity College at Cambridge, where he joined his older brothers Charles and Frederick. That same year, the brothers published *Poems by Two Brothers.* The collection of poems was published anonymously, and actually contained poems by all three men. The poems attracted the attention of a group of young men at Cambridge who were known as the Apostles, and Alfred Tennyson was invited to join this secret literary club. It was through this group that Tennyson met Arthur Hallam, who quickly became his closest friend. In 1829, Tennyson won the Chancellor's Medal for his poem "Timbuctoo," which was a great honor for the aspiring poet. The next year, Tennyson and Hallam traveled to Spain together as part of the rebel effort in opposition to Spain's King Ferdinand II. Tennyson's first major work, *Poems, Chiefly Lyrical,* which included the poem "Mariana," was published in 1830 and was well received.

Tennyson's father died in 1831. In order to help support his family, Tennyson left Cambridge without getting his degree. Tennyson traveled to the continent again with Hallam, who had become engaged to Tennyson's younger sister Emily. When they returned to England, Tennyson published a new collection, known simply as *Poems*. This collection included "The Lady of Shallot," which is one of Tennyson's most famous poems. At the time, however, critics panned the volume. Tennyson was devastated by the criticism. While dealing with the apparent failure of his book, Tennyson received word that Hallam had died while on holiday with his father in Vienna. Tennyson and his entire family were heartbroken, and in his grief, Tennyson began to write "In Memoriam" for his friend.

After a period of fierce grieving, Tennyson began to woo Emily Sellwood, whom he had known since childhood and who was the sister of his brother Charles's wife. Unfortunately, a bad investment left him in dire financial straits in 1840, and the engagement was called off. In 1842, a new collection in two volumes, also called *Poems,* was published, and this time, the critics raved. The collection *The Princess* was published in 1842. This collection, which included the now-famous "Ulysses" and "Tithonus," also received positive reviews, and Tennyson began to be well known in literary circles.

In 1850, Tennyson published "In Memoriam" to great acclaim. According to Professor James D. Kissane, the poem moved everyone who read it: "Probably no other poem in English has made so prodigious an impression on contemporary readers."[1] He was named to succeed William Wordsworth as England's poet laureate, in part

FACTS

The Poet Laureate

In the United Kingdom, the poet laureate is a poet whom the British monarchy appoints to write poems for special events, such as state funerals or occasions important to the royal family. The poet laureate is usually a well-known and highly respected poet who, once appointed, holds the position of poet laureate for the rest of his or her life. Some notable British poet laureates include Edmund Spenser, William Wordsworth, and Alfred, Lord Tennyson. From 1999 to 2009, Andrew Motion has been the poet laureate. His tenure had been notable, since it is the first laureateship to have a ten-year time limit. Other countries—and even individual states—also have poet laureates. The responsibilities of the poet laureate differ from country to country.

because Queen Victoria's husband, Prince Albert, had admired "In Memoriam."[2] That year, he also finally married Emily Sellwood. Two years later, their son Hallam was born, and was named after Tennyson's late friend; their son Lionel was born two years later in 1854. In 1853, the Tennysons moved to Farringford in the town of Freshwater on the Isle of Wight. Later, they built a summer home known as Aldworth, in Sussex.

Tennyson's fame and success grew after he was named poet laureate. In late 1854, he published "The Charge of the Light Brigade," which helped to motivate British troops during the Crimean War against Russia. In 1855, *Maud, and Other Poems* was published, and in 1859, Tennyson published the first edition of *Idylls of the King,* which tells the legends of King Arthur and Camelot. Four years later, Tennyson added a dedication poem to the epic story in honor of Prince Albert, who had died in 1861. Queen Victoria greatly appreciated this dedication, and she bestowed the title of baron on Tennyson in 1883.

Tennyson wrote all through the latter part of his life, and he died at the age of eighty-three on October 6, 1892, with a volume of Shakespeare in his hand. Amidst throngs of admirers, including some of the most notable writers, artists, and politicians of the day, Tennyson was buried in Westminster Abbey in Poets' Corner. Today, he is considered to be one of the greatest of the Victorian poets.

Ulysses

It little profits that an idle king,
By this still hearth, among these barren crags,
Matched with an aged wife, I mete and dole
Unequal laws unto a savage race,
That hoard, and sleep, and feed, and know not me.
I cannot rest from travel; I will drink
Life to the lees. All times I have enjoyed
Greatly, have suffered greatly, both with those
That loved me, and alone; on shore, and when
Through scudding drifts the rainy Hyades
Vext the dim sea. I am become a name;
For always roaming with a hungry heart
Much have I seen and known—cities of men
And manners, climates, councils, governments,
Myself not least, but honored of them all,—
And drunk delight of battle with my peers,
Far on the ringing plains of windy Troy.
I am a part of all that I have met;
Yet all experience is an arch wherethrough
Gleams that untraveled world whose margin fades
For ever and for ever when I move.
How dull it is to pause, to make an end,
To rust unburnished, not to shine in use!
As though to breathe were life! Life piled on life
Were all too little, and of one to me
Little remains; but every hour is saved
From that eternal silence, something more,
A bringer of new things; and vile it were
For some three suns to store and hoard myself,
And this gray spirit yearning in desire
To follow knowledge like a sinking star,
Beyond the utmost bound of human thought.
This is my son, mine own Telemachus,
To whom I leave the scepter and the isle,
Well-loved of me, discerning to fulfill
This labor, by slow prudence to make mild

A rugged people, and through soft degrees
Subdue them to the useful and the good.
Most blameless is he, centered in the sphere
Of common duties, decent not to fail
In offices of tenderness, and pay
Meet adoration to my household gods,
When I am gone. He works his work, I mine.
There lies the port; the vessel puffs her sail;
There gloom the dark, broad seas. My mariners,
Souls that have toiled, and wrought, and thought with me,
That ever with a frolic welcome took
The thunder and the sunshine, and opposed
Free hearts, free foreheads—you and I are old;
Old age hath yet his honor and his toil.
Death closes all; but something ere the end,
Some work of noble note, may yet be done,
Not unbecoming men that strove with gods.
The lights begin to twinkle from the rocks;
The long day wanes; the slow moon climbs; the deep
Moans round with many voices. Come, my friends,
'Tis not too late to seek a newer world.
Push off, and sitting well in order smite
The sounding furrows; for my purpose holds
To sail beyond the sunset, and the baths
Of all the western stars, until I die.
It may be that the gulfs will wash us down;
It may be we shall touch the Happy Isles,
And see the great Achilles, whom we knew.
Though much is taken, much abides; and though
We are not now that strength which in old days
Moved earth and heaven, that which we are, we are,
One equal temper of heroic hearts,
Made weak by time and fate, but strong in will
To strive, to seek, to find, and not to yield.

mete—to administer justice or punishment
lees—sediment or residue left over at the bottom of a bottle or glass of wine
Hyades—A group of stars in that were believed to foreshadow rain

The Eagle

He clasps the crag with crooked hands;
Close to the sun in lonely lands,
Ringed with the azure world, he stands.
The wrinkled sea beneath him crawls;
He watches from his mountain walls,
And like a thunderbolt he falls.

crag—a rugged mass of a rock pointing upward

azure—a light purplish blue, as in the color of the
   sky

Discussion Questions

1. How does Tennyson use the eagle's viewpoint to describe the landscape?

2. How is the eagle's power illustrated, and to what end?

Dedication: Idylls of the King

These to His Memory—since he held them dear,
Perchance as finding there unconsciously
Some image of himself—I dedicate,
I dedicate, I consecrate with tears—
These Idylls.

And indeed He seems to me
Scarce other than my king's ideal knight,
'Who reverenced his conscience as his king;
Whose glory was, redressing human wrong;
Who spake no slander, no, nor listened to it;
Who loved one only and who clave to her—'
Her—over all whose realms to their last isle,
Commingled with the gloom of imminent war,
The shadow of His loss drew like eclipse,
Darkening the world. We have lost him: he is gone:
We know him now: all narrow jealousies
Are silent; and we see him as he moved,
How modest, kindly, all-accomplished, wise,
With what sublime repression of himself,
And in what limits, and how tenderly;
Not swaying to this faction or to that;
Not making his high place the lawless perch
Of winged ambitions, nor a vantage-ground
For pleasure; but through all this tract of years
Wearing the white flower of a blameless life,
Before a thousand peering littlenesses,
In that fierce light which beats upon a throne,
And blackens every blot: for where is he,
Who dares foreshadow for an only son

A lovelier life, a more unstained, than his?
Or how should England dreaming of his sons
Hope more for these than some inheritance
Of such a life, a heart, a mind as thine,
Thou noble Father of her Kings to be,
Laborious for her people and her poor—
Voice in the rich dawn of an ampler day—
Far-sighted summoner of War and Waste
To fruitful strifes and rivalries of peace—
Sweet nature gilded by the gracious gleam
Of letters, dear to Science, dear to Art,
Dear to thy land and ours, a Prince indeed,
Beyond all titles, and a household name,
Hereafter, through all times, Albert the Good.

Break not, O woman's-heart, but still endure;
Break not, for thou art Royal, but endure,
Remembering all the beauty of that star
Which shone so close beside Thee that ye made
One light together, but has past and leaves
The Crown a lonely splendour.

May all love,
His love, unseen but felt, o'ershadow Thee,
The love of all Thy sons encompass Thee,
The love of all Thy daughters cherish Thee,
The love of all Thy people comfort Thee,
Till God's love set Thee at his side again!

my king—King Arthur

thy land—Prince Albert was from Saxe-Coburg, which is now in Germany

Comments

The *Idylls of the King* is Tennyson's famous cycle of poems telling the stories of King Arthur and Camelot. The cycle was published in pieces between 1859 and 1885, and the Dedication was published in 1862, soon after the death of Prince Albert, the Prince Consort, Queen Victoria's beloved husband. The poem is directed to the Prince Albert and "His Memory."

Discussion Questions

1. Why might Prince Albert have been one of King Arthur's most ideal knights, according to the poem? What language suggests this and why?

2. By the time the dedication was published, Tennyson was already the poet laureate. What impact might this dedication have on a reading of the *Idylls* in general, and why?

Read More

Blume, Lesley M. M. *Tennyson.* New York: Alfred A. Knopf, 2008.

Tennyson, Alfred. *The Lady of Shalott,* Toronto: Kids Can Press, 2005.

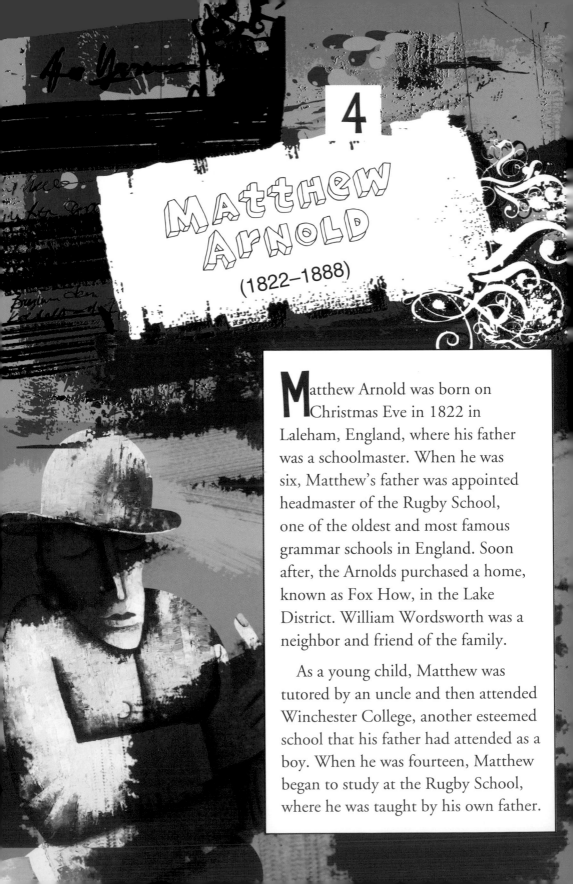

4

MATTHEW ARNOLD

(1822–1888)

Matthew Arnold was born on Christmas Eve in 1822 in Laleham, England, where his father was a schoolmaster. When he was six, Matthew's father was appointed headmaster of the Rugby School, one of the oldest and most famous grammar schools in England. Soon after, the Arnolds purchased a home, known as Fox How, in the Lake District. William Wordsworth was a neighbor and friend of the family.

As a young child, Matthew was tutored by an uncle and then attended Winchester College, another esteemed school that his father had attended as a boy. When he was fourteen, Matthew began to study at the Rugby School, where he was taught by his own father.

While at Rugby, Matthew began to write poetry, which he shared with his family, and he won an award for his poem "Alaric at Rome."

After Rugby, Arnold went to Oxford University, where he was a student in Balliol College. In 1842, while Arnold was at Oxford, his father died of heart disease at the age of forty-seven. Arnold

Matthew Arnold

continued his education, although he was not particularly serious. As his closest friend Arthur Hugh Clough wrote: "Matt is full of Parisianism; Theatre in general, and Rachel (a famous actress) in special... his hair is guiltless of English scissors: he breakfasts at 12 ... and in the week ... he has been to Chapel once."[1] A voracious reader as well as a budding poet, Arnold won the prestigious Newdigate Prize for "Cromwell, A Prize Poem" in 1843.

Upon receiving his degree from Oxford in 1844, Arnold taught briefly at Rugby and was soon elected a Fellow of Oriel College at Oxford, a distinction once held by his father. In 1847, he became the private secretary to Lord Lansdowne, an influential statesman. He traveled to Switzerland in 1848 and 1849, where he presumably met the woman whom he immortalized in his poetry as "Marguerite." In 1849, Arnold's first volume of poems, *The Strayed Reveller and Other Poems,* was published, though the work received little recognition.

In 1851, Landsdowne helped Arnold secure a position as a school inspector, a post he would hold for more than thirty years. It was a tiring job, which Arnold took in order to gain a secure income that would allow him to marry. He later said, "Though I am a schoolmaster's son, I confess that school-teaching or school-inspecting is not the line of life I should naturally have chosen. I adopted it in order to marry a lady.... But the irksomeness of my new duties was what I felt most, and during the first year or so it was sometimes insupportable."[2]

The income from the school inspector position allowed Arnold to marry Frances Lucy Wightman, daughter of Sir William Wightman, a judge. It was a happy marriage, and the couple had six children. Tragically, two of their sons—Basil, age two, and Thomas, age sixteen—died in 1868 in unrelated incidents. Another son, William, died at age eighteen in 1872.

In 1852, Arnold published *Empedocles on Etna, and Other Poems.* In 1853, he published *Poems: A New Edition.* Notably, this collection did not include "Empedocles on Etna," although today, it is considered to be one of his most important works. In 1854, Arnold published a new edition of his poems, though there was only one major new poem in the collection, the poem "Balder Dead."

In 1857, Arnold became a professor of Poetry at Oxford, a position he held for ten years. His tenure at Oxford was notable, since he gave his lectures in English rather than in Latin, as had been the norm. During this time, he continued his work as a school inspector and he began to write essays on literary and social criticism. Although he did publish a collection entitled *New Poems* in 1867, in which he restored "Empedocles on Etna" at Robert Browning's request, his work as a critic soon took prominence in his writing. Some of his most famous critical works include *Essays in Criticism* (1865), *Culture and Anarchy* (1869), and *Literature and Dogma* (1873).

In 1883, Arnold received a pension so that he could retire from his post as school inspector. He traveled to the United States, where he gave a series of lectures on education and Ralph Waldo Emerson, and he traveled as far west as St. Louis. During this trip, his daughter Lucy met and fell in love with an American, whom she eventually married. In 1888, Arnold went to meet Lucy who was coming to visit, and he died suddenly of a heart attack while running to catch a tram. He is buried in Laleham, Middlesex, and is recognized with a bust in Poets' Corner, Westminster Abbey.

Dover Beach

The sea is calm tonight.
The tide is full, the moon lies fair
Upon the straits; on the French coast, the light
Gleams and is gone; the cliffs of England stand,
Glimmering and vast, out in the tranquil bay.
Come to the window, sweet is the night-air!
Only, from the long line of spray
Where the sea meets the moon-blanched land,

Listen! you hear the grating roar
Of pebbles which the waves draw back, and fling,
At their return, up the high strand,
Begin, and cease, and then again begin,
With tremulous cadence slow, and bring
The eternal note of sadness in.

Sophocles long ago
Heard it on the Aegean, and it brought
Into his mind the turbid ebb and flow
Of human misery; we
Find also in the sound a thought,
Hearing it by this distant northern sea.

The Sea of Faith
Was once, too, at the full, and round earth's shore

Lay like the folds of a bright girdle furled.
But now I only hear
Its melancholy, long, withdrawing roar,
Retreating, to the breath
Of the night-wind, down the vast edges drear
And naked shingles of the world.

Ah, love, let us be true
To one another! for the world, which seems
To lie before us like a land of dreams,
So various, so beautiful, so new,
Hath really neither joy, nor love, nor light,
Nor certitude, nor peace, nor help for pain;
And we are here as on a darkling plain
Swept with confused alarms of struggle and flight,
Where ignorant armies clash by night.

blanched—whitened.

Sophocles—a Greek playwright who lived in the fifth century B.C.E.
He is one of three writers of Greek tragedy whose works survived
till today (the others are Aeschylus and Euripides). His surviving
plays include *Oedipus the King* and *Antigone.*

Aegean—the part of the Mediterranean Sea that lies between Greece
and Turkey

turbid—cloudy

girdle—belt

shingles—small round pebbles

Summary and Explication: "Dover Beach"

Probably Matthew Arnold's most famous poem, "Dover Beach" was first published in 1867, although it was written earlier. In the poem, while the sea is seemingly calm in the opening stanza, the speaker hears the roar of the waves in the distance, and the ebb and flow of the tide suggest inevitable change and the erosion of time. "The eternal note of sadness" soon pervades the poem's tone, despite the serenity of the opening lines. History is evoked with the reference to Sophocles, who the speaker says would have heard a similar sadness in the waves of the Aegean Sea. While at one point, there was a spark of hope in the "Sea of Faith," that faith is now gone and all that remains is a deafening roar. The speaker ultimately turns back to his beloved and suggests that they "be true / To one another." By focusing on each other, they will be able to live within the world which "Hath really neither joy, nor love, nor light, / Nor certitude, nor peace, nor help for pain." They must struggle on, with each other, in a world in which confusion reigns, as emphasized by the increasingly harsh lines ending with "Where ignorant armies clash by night." This closing metaphor of armies fighting on an open plain at night is probably an allusion to Thucydides' history of the Peloponnesian War in which a battle was fought on a cliff top in the dark. The confusion was so significant that the soldiers did not know if they were fighting their comrades or their enemies. By drawing attention to this battle, Arnold highlights the current state of confusion in the world, a confusion into which the speaker—and the reader—are drawn regardless of whether or not they want to dive into the fray.

Techniques and Devices

A metaphor is a figure of speech in which a word or a phrase is used to represent something else. The idea of a poorly lit battle as a metaphor for the world's confusion was discussed above.

FACTS

The Lake District

The Lake District is an area in northwest England in the county of Cumbria that has been famous as a vacation destination for centuries. The region has numerous lakes and mountains, or "fells," and is considered to be one of the most beautiful parts of the United Kingdom. The poet William Wordsworth lived in the region for most of his life, and he was known as one of the Lake Poets, along with Samuel Coleridge and Robert Southey. Wordsworth published a guidebook of the area in 1810 that helped to popularize the area in the nineteenth century. Many writers of the time either visited the Lake District or lived there themselves, including Alfred, Lord Tennyson and Matthew Arnold.

A simile, on the other hand, is a comparison of different things using the words "like" or "as." In this poem, similes include "the world … before us like a land of dreams" and "the Sea of Faith lay … like the folds of a bright girdle furled."

Interpretation

"Dover Beach" is often regarded as a description of the crisis in faith prevalent in Victorian society, a crisis brought on by Charles Darwin's theory of evolution, the Industrial Revolution, and controversies within the Church of England. By comparing the past and the present, Arnold illustrates that the "grating roar," or the confusion, may seem new but is, in fact, a part of the human condition.

Discussion Questions

1. What lines in this poem depict despair? How do they do this?

2. Is there any hope for mankind suggested in this poem? Why or why not?

To Marguerite

Yes! in the sea of life enisled,
With echoing straits between us thrown,
Dotting the shoreless watery wild,
We mortal millions live alone.
The islands feel the enclasping flow,
And then their endless bounds they know.

But when the moon their hollows lights,
And they are swept by balms of spring,
And in their glens, on starry nights,
The nightingales divinely sing;
And lovely notes, from shore to shore,
Across the sounds and channels pour—

Oh! then a longing like despair
Is to their farthest caverns sent;
For surely once, they feel, we were
Parts of a single continent!
Now round us spreads the watery plain—
Oh, might our marges meet again!

Who ordered, that their longing's fire
Should be, as soon as kindled, cooled?
Who renders vain their deep desire?—
A god, a god their severance ruled!
And bade betwixt their shores to be
The unplumbed, salt, estranging sea.

enisled—isolated, as if on an island

marges—margin

renders vain—makes worthless

severance—separation

Comments

Marguerite seems to have been a French girl whom Matthew Arnold met and fell in love with while in Switzerland before marrying his wife. He wrote three poems to her; these are part of a sequence of poems known as his "Switzerland" poems.

Discussion Questions

1. How is the metaphor of the sea used in this poem? Does the metaphor change? How and to what effect?

2. How does the speaker describe his love for Marguerite? What words are used to describe his despair? How does this contrast impact the tone of the poem?

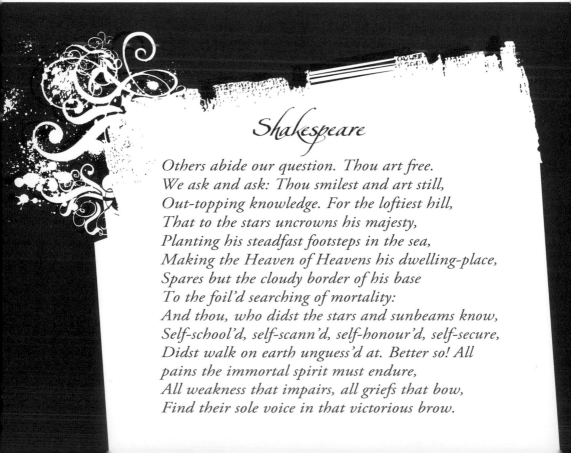

Shakespeare

Others abide our question. Thou art free.
We ask and ask: Thou smilest and art still,
Out-topping knowledge. For the loftiest hill,
That to the stars uncrowns his majesty,
Planting his steadfast footsteps in the sea,
Making the Heaven of Heavens his dwelling-place,
Spares but the cloudy border of his base
To the foil'd searching of mortality:
And thou, who didst the stars and sunbeams know,
Self-school'd, self-scann'd, self-honour'd, self-secure,
Didst walk on earth unguess'd at. Better so! All
pains the immortal spirit must endure,
All weakness that impairs, all griefs that bow,
Find their sole voice in that victorious brow.

Discussion QuesTion

1. How does Arnold compare Shakespeare as an individual with Shakespeare as a cultural icon?

2. This poem is a sonnet, a kind of a poem for which Shakespeare is famous. What is the impact of this form on your reading of this poem?

Read More

Collini, Stefan. *Matthew Arnold: A Critical Portrait.* New York: Oxford University Press, 2008.

Gottfried, Leon Albert. *Matthew Arnold and the Romantics.* Lincoln: University of Nebraska Press, 1963.

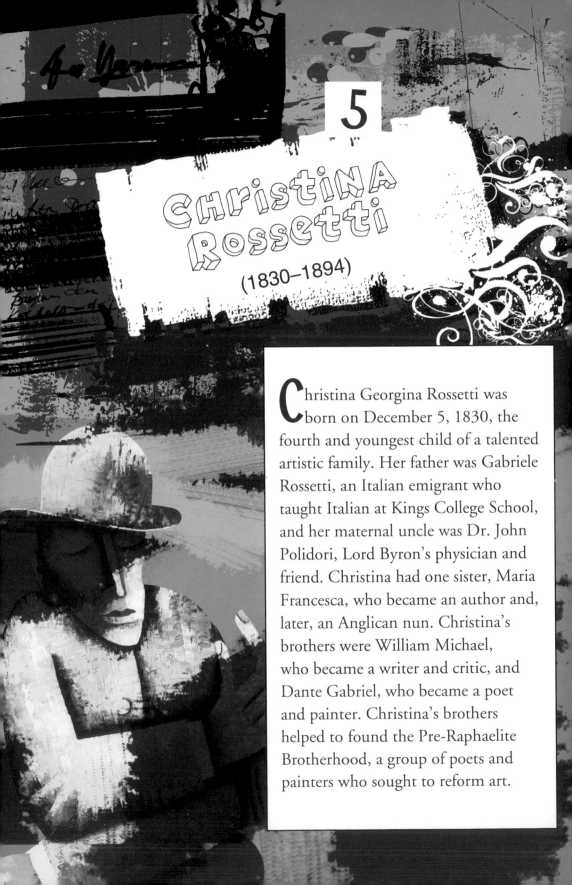

5

Christina Rossetti

(1830–1894)

Christina Georgina Rossetti was born on December 5, 1830, the fourth and youngest child of a talented artistic family. Her father was Gabriele Rossetti, an Italian emigrant who taught Italian at Kings College School, and her maternal uncle was Dr. John Polidori, Lord Byron's physician and friend. Christina had one sister, Maria Francesca, who became an author and, later, an Anglican nun. Christina's brothers were William Michael, who became a writer and critic, and Dante Gabriel, who became a poet and painter. Christina's brothers helped to found the Pre-Raphaelite Brotherhood, a group of poets and painters who sought to reform art.

Christina Rossetti

Sappho

I sigh at day-dawn, and I sigh
When the dull day is passing by.
I sigh at evening, and again
I sigh when night brings sleep to men.
Oh! it were better far to die
Than thus for ever mourn and sigh,
And in death's dreamless sleep to be
Unconscious that none weep for me;
Eased from my weight of heaviness,
Forgetful of forgetfulness,
Resting from pain and care and sorrow
Thro' the long night that knows no morrow;
Living unloved, to die unknown,
Unwept, untended and alone.

Summary and Explication: "Sappho"

Born on the island of Lesbos in the seventh century B.C.E., Sappho was a Greek poet whose work achieved great fame in antiquity. Today, only fragments of her poems survive. These focus mainly on sensuality, love, and friendship between women. Today, references to Sappho and Lesbos often bring to mind erotic love between women, although this emphasis excludes other significant elements of her writing and mythology. Since antiquity, Sappho has often been referred to as a muse, or an individual who inspires art, for both men and women; in Rossetti's time, Sappho was especially celebrated as one of the most important women poets of all time. Although little is actually known about Sappho's life, one legend suggests that she killed herself by jumping off a cliff because of her love for a ferryman.

In this poem, the speaker is Sappho, who is distraught because she loves someone, but this love is not returned. In the first four lines,

Discussion Questions

1. What is the speaker's attitude toward the reader? Why do you think this?

2. How are the seasons used as a metaphor in this poem?

FACTS

The Pre-Raphaelite Brotherhood

Founded in 1849, the Pre-Raphaelite Brotherhood was a group of artists officially made up of James Collinson, William Holman Hunt, John Everett Millais, Dante Gabriel Rossetti, William Michael Rossetti, Frederic George Stephens, and Thomas Woolner. The group was heavily influenced by the romantic movement in literature. The Pre-Raphaelite Brotherhood abhorred what they considered to be the mechanistic approach to art after the great Renaissance painters Raphael and Michelangelo. The work of the Pre-Raphaelite Brotherhood artists involved vivid colors and detail and focused on medieval themes or legends. They were dedicated to experimenting with artistic conventions, especially in contrast to what was being taught at the Royal Academy of Arts, where some were students. The group published a literary magazine called *The Germ*. Christina Rossetti was part of the inner circle of the brotherhood, though not officially a member.

This painting by Dante Gabriel Rossetti exemplifies the Pre-Raphaelite style.

Excerpt from
Goblin Market

Backwards up the mossy glen
Turned and trooped the goblin men,
With their shrill repeated cry,
"Come buy, come buy."
When they reached where Laura was
They stood stock still upon the moss,
Leering at each other,
Brother with queer brother;
Signalling each other,
Brother with sly brother.
One set his basket down,
One reared his plate;
One began to weave a crown
Of tendrils, leaves, and rough nuts brown
(Men sell not such in any town);
One heaved the golden weight
Of dish and fruit to offer her:
"Come buy, come buy," was still their cry.
Laura stared but did not stir,
Longed but had no money:
The whisk-tailed merchant bade her taste
In tones as smooth as honey,
The cat-faced purr'd,
The rat-paced spoke a word
Of welcome, and the snail-paced even was heard;
One parrot-voiced and jolly
Cried "Pretty Goblin" still for "Pretty Polly;"—
One whistled like a bird.

But sweet-tooth Laura spoke in haste:
"Good folk, I have no coin;

To take were to purloin:
I have no copper in my purse,
I have no silver either,
And all my gold is on the furze
That shakes in windy weather
Above the rusty heather."
"You have much gold upon your head,"
They answered all together:
"Buy from us with a golden curl."
She clipped a precious golden lock,
She dropped a tear more rare than pearl,
Then sucked their fruit globes fair or red:
Sweeter than honey from the rock,
Stronger than man-rejoicing wine,
Clearer than water flowed that juice;
She never tasted such before,
How should it cloy with length of use?
She sucked and sucked and sucked the more
Fruits which that unknown orchard bore,
She sucked until her lips were sore;
Then flung the emptied rinds away
But gathered up one kernel-stone,
And knew not was it night or day
As she turned home alone.

Lizzie met her at the gate
Full of wise upbraidings:
"Dear, you should not stay so late,
Twilight is not good for maidens;
Should not loiter in the glen
In the haunts of goblin men.
Do you not remember Jeanie,
How she met them in the moonlight,
Took their gifts both choice and many,

Ate their fruits and wore their flowers
Plucked from bowers
Where summer ripens at all hours?
But ever in the moonlight
She pined and pined away;
Sought them by night and day,
Found them no more but dwindled and grew grey;
Then fell with the first snow,
While to this day no grass will grow
Where she lies low:
I planted daisies there a year ago
That never blow.
You should not loiter so."
"Nay, hush," said Laura:
"Nay, hush, my sister:
I ate and ate my fill,
Yet my mouth waters still…"

cloy—to become distasteful through excess

Summary and Explication: "Goblin Market"

In this poem, two sisters are walking in the woods when they hear the goblins' cries. Laura is seduced by their offerings of delicious fruits, and against the warnings of her sister, Lizzie, she buys their wares by trading a lock of her hair. She feasts on the fruit and returns home. Soon after, she finds herself craving the fruit again. She falls into despair when she realizes that she is no longer able to hear the cries of the goblin men. Lizzie watches her sister begin to die and one night, she seeks out the goblin men. Lizzie offers the men a coin to buy some fruit and take it back to her sister. The goblins refuse to let her take the fruit with her. Rather, they insist that she eat it in their presence, and they attack her when she refuses. In the attack, Lizzie is covered with the fruit juice and when she returns to her sister, she tells her to "Eat me, drink me, love me." Laura does so, and the next morning, she wakes up revived. The sisters grow up to have children of their own whom they warn against the evils of the goblin men.

Discussion Questions

1. How does Rossetti describe Laura's feast, and how does this contrast with her desire at the end of this selection?

2. Compare the descriptions of the goblins to the language describing Laura in this excerpt. What does this comparison suggest?

Read More

Des Cars, Laurence. *The Pre-Raphaelites: Romance and Realism.* New York: Abrams Discoveries, 2000.

W.B. YEATS

(1865–1939)

William Butler Yeats was born on June 13, 1865, in Sandymount, County Dublin, Ireland. He was the eldest of six children born to John Butler Yeats and Susan Mary Pollexfen Yeats, both from relatively well-to-do Anglo-Protestant families. After William's birth, the family moved frequently, in part because John Butler Yeats decided to abandon a plan to study law in favor of studying art (he eventually became a well-known painter). The family first moved to London, but soon they were traveling back and forth to County Sligo in Ireland where they stayed with Susan Yeats's family. During this time, the family was relatively poor and dependent on the generosity of Susan Yeats's parents and siblings.

When the children were young, they were educated at home by their father and, in Sligo, by a series of governesses. When he was eleven, William was sent to the Godolphin School in London. He was a poor student and had a lot of trouble with reading. In late 1881, the family moved back to Ireland. Here, William attended Erasmus Smith High School in Dublin. It was during this time that

William Butler Yeats

William first began to write. By the time he left high school, his early trouble with reading was long gone, and he had read the work of Percy Bysshe Shelley, William Blake, and Matthew Arnold.

The late 1880s were a time of change in Ireland. Independence from British rule was the subject of debate in all groups—from the Catholic tenant farmers to Anglo-Irish Protestants like Yeats and his family. Yeats's immediate family was decidedly pro-Irish, in contrast to some of their relatives. Soon, Yeats was attending events at the Young Ireland Society. In the late 1880s, Yeats began a lifelong pursuit of mysticism and the occult, which was fast becoming a popular interest throughout Europe.

FACTS

The Irish Conflict

In the midst of the First World War, Irish nationalists rebelled against the British in Dublin on Easter Sunday 1916. The rebellion was short lived, and the British executed the leaders of the uprising. Although the British intended this action to quash future rebellion, the executions actually served to rally the Irish. The Anglo-Irish conflict continued to boil throughout World War I. In 1922, Ireland was divided between its mostly Catholic South and mostly Protestant North. The South was established as the Irish Free State, which was a "dominion" of the United Kingdom. This status meant that it was still part of the British Commonwealth. The Republic of Ireland did not gain full independence from Britain until 1948, and the region experienced unrest throughout most of the twentieth century.

In 1887, Yeats moved with his family back to London. In 1889, he published *The Wanderings of Oisin and Other Poems,* a series of poems focused on Irish mythology that was recognized as a strong first collection. Almost as significant as this first publication, however, was Yeats's meeting with Maud Gonne, a beautiful, free-spirited young English heiress who was an ardent Irish nationalist. Yeats quickly fell in love, but his feelings were not returned. Yeats's infatuation with Gonne continued for decades, despite the fact that she had two children with another man. Yeats was so obsessed that he proposed marriage several times, and continued to admire her, even after she married a militant nationalist.

In 1890, while still living in London, Yeats helped to create the Rhymers' Club, a group of poets who met regularly to read and discuss their poems. During this time, Yeats traveled back and forth between Ireland and London. He wrote prolifically and published new collections of poetry regularly. He also continued to develop his talents and interest in plays, especially those written in verse. He joined with Lady Augusta Gregory and Edward Martyn to found the Irish Literary Theatre, of which Yeats was the first president. This theatre was part of an overall revival of nationalistic efforts in Ireland around the turn of the century. In the theatre's manifesto, Yeats wrote: "We hope to find in Ireland an uncorrupted & imaginative audience trained to listen by its passion for oratory, & believe that our desire to bring upon the stage the deeper thoughts & … emotions of Ireland will ensure for us a tolerant welcome."[1] With the support of a patron, the society was able to open the Abbey Theatre in 1904.

For much of the next decade, Yeats focused his energy on managing and writing for the Abbey Theatre. He also wrote constantly and traveled to the United States several times. In 1914, World War I began, throwing the world into turmoil, which Yeats felt firsthand when Major Robert Gregory, Lady Gregory's son, was killed in action in 1918. His death inspired Yeats's famous poem, "An Irish Airman Foresees His Death." Ireland was undergoing violent changes itself. The Easter Rising of 1916—which inspired Yeats's "Easter 1916"—led to the establishment of the Irish Republic. After the Easter Rising, Yeats lived mainly in Ireland, though he continued to travel frequently.

In 1917, Yeats married George (Georgie) Hyde-Lees, with whom he shared a passionate interest in mysticism and the occult. She was twenty-four and he was fifty-two. It seems to have been a happy marriage, and the couple had two children: Anne Butler Yeats, born in 1919, and William Michael (known as Michael), born in 1921.

Yeats was appointed to the new Irish Senate in 1922, and to a second term two years later. He was awarded the Nobel Prize for literature in 1923. In his Nobel lecture, Yeats spoke of the Irish Literary Theatre and how the challenges of building the theatre helped to define the Irish culture as it was developing in the early twentieth century: "We were to find ourselves in a quarrel with public opinion that compelled us against our own will and the will of our players to become always more realistic, substituting dialect for verse, common speech for dialect."[2]

In his later years, Yeats continued to be active in Irish politics, though he resigned his Senate seat in 1928 because of poor health. He wrote prolifically, and though his subject matter ranged widely, he was not swayed from traditional forms of poetry. Yeats died on January 28, 1939, in France and was buried in Roquebrune-Cap-Martin. Following his wishes, his body was disinterred and moved in 1948. He was reburied in Drumcliff, in County Sligo, Ireland. Lines from one of his poems "Under Ben Bulben" were inscribed on his grave: "Cast a cold Eye / On Life, on Death / Horseman, pass by."

The Second Coming

Turning and turning in the widening gyre
The falcon cannot hear the falconer;
Things fall apart; the centre cannot hold;
Mere anarchy is loosed upon the world,
The blood-dimmed tide is loosed, and everywhere
The ceremony of innocence is drowned;
The best lack all conviction, while the worst
Are full of passionate intensity.

Surely some revelation is at hand;
Surely the Second Coming is at hand.
The Second Coming! Hardly are those words out
When a vast image out of Spiritus Mundi
Troubles my sight: somewhere in sands of the desert
A shape with lion body and the head of a man,
A gaze blank and pitiless as the sun,
Is moving its slow thighs, while all about it
Reel shadows of the indignant desert birds.
The darkness drops again; but now I know
That twenty centuries of stony sleep
Were vexed to nightmare by a rocking cradle,
And what rough beast, its hour come round at last,
Slouches towards Bethlehem to be born?

gyre—whirl or spiral, as of a falcon around its trainer

Spiritus Mundi—literally, "the spirit of the world," i.e.,
       the collective consciousness

reel—to sway or stagger

Summary and Explication: "The Second Coming"

One of Yeats's most famous poems, "The Second Coming" was first published in 1920. The title refers to the Apocalypse, the end of the world as described in the Bible. In the poems's first stanza, the reader sees images of the world as it is in the present. A falcon turns in an ever-widening spiral around the falconer, its trainer, and the bird can no longer hear the falconer's voice. As the spiral gets larger and larger, its form becomes less certain. Soon, its "centre," the falconer, will not "hold," or be able to retain control over the falcon. When the falconer loses control, the falcon will no longer be tame and will return to an uncontrolled, animalistic state. Anarchy will come over the world, and those at both ends of the human spectrum, "the best" and "the worst," will falter. The second stanza shows what the world will be like when the "gyre" in the first stanza collapses, an image that is inspired by the "*Spiritus Mundi,*" or the spirit of the world.

Techniques and Devices

In its simplest definition, imagery is the pictures that are brought to mind from words. Here Yeats evokes biblical and mythological images as a means of suggesting a looming apocalypse.

Interpretation

"The Second Coming" is often read as a commentary on the state of civilization in the wake of World War I and the years of unrest in Ireland. By suggesting that the apocalypse will come in the form of a sphinx ("A shape with lion body and the head of a man"), the poem offers a contrast between the modern world and the ancient world. This sphinx, which has been sleeping for "twenty centuries," or the two millennia of Christianity, is about to have its time come "round" again, and the poem warns of impending doom for civilization.

DiscussiON QuesTioNS

1. Why do you think Yeats used the phrase "ceremony of innocence" in the first stanza, rather than just "innocence"?

2. What is the meaning of the "rocking cradle" in the second stanza?

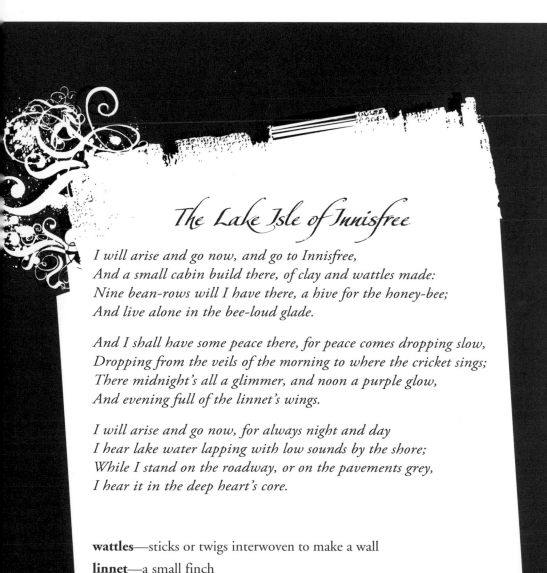

The Lake Isle of Innisfree

I will arise and go now, and go to Innisfree,
And a small cabin build there, of clay and wattles made:
Nine bean-rows will I have there, a hive for the honey-bee;
And live alone in the bee-loud glade.

And I shall have some peace there, for peace comes dropping slow,
Dropping from the veils of the morning to where the cricket sings;
There midnight's all a glimmer, and noon a purple glow,
And evening full of the linnet's wings.

I will arise and go now, for always night and day
I hear lake water lapping with low sounds by the shore;
While I stand on the roadway, or on the pavements grey,
I hear it in the deep heart's core.

wattles—sticks or twigs interwoven to make a wall
linnet—a small finch

Discussion Questions

1. Innisfree is a small island near Sligo in northwestern Ireland. By positioning the speaker in the city at the end of the poem, what does this poem suggest about the impact of Innisfree on the speaker's "deep heart's core"?

2. What language suggests a sense of calm in Innisfree? How does the rhythm of the poem reinforce this?

An Irish Airman Foresees His Death

I know that I shall meet my fate
Somewhere among the clouds above;
Those that I fight I do not hate,
Those that I guard I do not love;
My country is Kiltartan Cross,
My countrymen Kiltartan's poor,
No likely end could bring them loss
Or leave them happier than before.
Nor law, nor duty bade me fight,
Nor public men, nor cheering crowds,
A lonely impulse of delight
Drove to this tumult in the clouds;
I balanced all, brought all to mind,
The years to come seemed waste of breath,
A waste of breath the years behind
In balance with this life, this death.

Kiltartan Cross—an area in County Galway, Ireland,
    where Lady Augusta Gregory lived

Discussion Questions

1. The airman says, "Those that I fight I do not hate, / Those that I guard I do not love." If this is true, why did the airman choose to enter the war?

2. Does the airman seem upset about his impending death? Why or why not?

Read More

Allison, Jonathan, editor. *William Butler Yeats*. New York: Sterling Publishing Company, 2002.

Yeats, W. B. *Fairy Tales of Ireland*. New York: Delacorte Press, 1990.

EDith Sitwell

(1887–1964)

Born on September 7, 1887, Edith Sitwell was the eldest child of Lady Ida and Sir George Sitwell, a baronet. She had two brothers, Osbert and Sacheverell, with whom she was very close. The children grew up on their parents' estate, Renishaw Hall in Derbyshire, which is still home to members of the Sitwell family. In childhood, Edith was educated at home by governesses. She was a sensitive, bookish girl who loved music and cared little for her mother's fashionable society, which caused significant tension between the two. In 1903, Helen Rootham became Edith's governess and a lifelong relationship was born. Rootham, an aspiring poet herself, introduced Edith to the work of French symbolist poets, which greatly affected Sitwell's work later in life.[1]

Just before World War I, Sitwell and Rootham moved to London together, and Sitwell established a salon, a regular meeting of artists and intellectuals. Her first published poem was "Drowned Suns," which came out in 1913. In 1915, she published her first collection of poetry, entitled *The Mother and Other Poems*. Soon after, Sitwell established the avant-garde literary anthology *Wheels*, which she edited and to which she and her brothers contributed poems. *Wheels* was published annually until 1921.

Sitwell was unusual in both looks and behavior. According to one account of her family's history, "She set her aquiline nose and long fingers off with sweeping fabrics and many large rings, and she involved herself in the world of literature and the arts with gusto."[2] Her eccentricity was well known, and in 1923, she furthered this reputation with a unique—and apparently bizarre—performance of her newest collection, *Façade*. At this event, which took place at London's Aeolian Hall, Sitwell read the various poems of the collection, which had been set to music by William Walton. This would not have been all that unusual, except that Sitwell recited the poems in a monotone through a megaphone from behind a painted curtain. According to editors Richard Ellman and Robert O'Clair, "The critics were generally baffled or exasperated...."[3] On the other hand, more than twenty years later, the work received positive responses when it was premiered at New York's Museum of Modern Art in 1949. Although the critical response to *Façade* was initially negative, the work helped to solidify Sitwell's place as a significant force in the artistic movement of the time. She became friends with such literary luminaries as Virginia Woolf and Gertrude Stein, among others.

In the early 1930s, Sitwell moved from London to Paris with
Rootham, who was ill with cancer. This was a decade of extremes
for Sitwell. On one hand, she received a medal of the Royal Society
of Literature in 1933, and during her time in Paris, she met many of
the era's most notable writers. Furthermore, it was during this time
that she met Bryher Ellerman, a wealthy British heiress who became
her patron and friend. On the other, Sitwell's mother passed away

Edith Sitwell

in 1937—Sitwell did not attend the funeral because of her strained relationship with her parents—and her companion Rootham died in 1938. Eventually, Sitwell left Europe to live at Renishaw Hall during most of World War II.

According to the journalist Joseph Pearce, "Edith Sitwell was a shock-trooper of the poetic avant garde, a champion of modernity who reveled in the use of shock tactics to push the boundaries of poetry, angering traditionalists in the process."[4] Dedicated to innovation in sound and rhythm, Sitwell's post-*Façade* poems focused on social issues more and more. During World War II, her famous poem "Still Falls the Rain" dramatically depicts the bombing of London. This poem was later set to music by the composer Benjamin Britten. Later works criticized issues of global suffering and the last work published in her lifetime, "The Outcasts," supported the reform of antihomosexuality laws in England.

Sitwell received honorary doctorates from the universities of Leeds and Durham, the University of Sheffield, and Oxford University, where she was the first woman to receive this distinction. In 1954, Sitwell was made a Dame of the Order of the British Empire. The following year, Sitwell officially converted to Catholicism; the novelist Evelyn Waugh was her godfather.

Sitwell died in London on December 9, 1964, at the age of seventy-seven. Her autobiography, *Taken Care Of,* was published posthumously. Although not widely popular today, according to Professor Robert K. Martin:

> Edith Sitwell needs to be remembered not only as the bright young parodist of *Façade*, but as the angry chronicler of social injustice, as a poet who has found forms adequate to the atomic age and its horrors, and as a foremost poet of love. Her work displays enormous range of subject and of form. With her contemporary [T. S.] Eliot she remains one of the most important voices of twentieth-century English poetry.[5]

Still Falls the Rain

The Raids, 1940.
Night and Dawn.

Still falls the Rain—
Dark as the world of man, black as our loss—
Blind as the nineteen hundred and forty nails
Upon the Cross.

Still falls the Rain

With a sound like the pulse of the heart that is changed to the hammer-beat
In the Potter's Field, and the sound of the impious feet
On the Tomb:

Still falls the Rain

In the Field of Blood where the small hopes breed and the human brain
Nurtures its greed, that worm with the brow of Cain.
Still falls the Rain
At the feet of the Starved Man hung upon the Cross.
Christ that each day, each night, nails there, have mercy on us—
On Dives and on Lazarus:
Under the Rain the sore and the gold are as one.

Still falls the Rain—
Still falls the Blood from the Starved Man's wounded Side:
He bears in His Heart all wounds—those of the light that died,
The last faint spark
In the self-murdered heart, the wounds of the sad uncomprehending dark,
The wounds of the baited bear—
The blind and weeping bear whom the keepers beat
On his helpless flesh… the tears of the hunted hare.

Still falls the Rain—
Then—O Ile leape up to my God: who pulles me doune—
See, see where Christ's blood streames in the firmament:
It flows from the Brow we nailed upon the tree
Deep to the dying, to the thirsting heart
That holds the fires of the world—dark-smirched with pain
As Caesar's laurel crown.

Then sounds the voice of One who like the heart of man
Was once a child who among beasts has lain—
"Still do I love, still shed my innocent light, my Blood, for thee."

raids—during World War II, the German air force bombed London regularly, causing massive damage and thousands of casualties.

Potter's Field—a cemetery for foreigners and the poor. The term comes from the Bible (Matthew 27:7), which tells of a cemetery outside of Jerusalem that was purchased with the money acquired by Judas after his betrayal of Jesus. It was also called the Field of Blood because the money was considered blood money.

Cain—the elder son of Adam and Eve, who killed his brother Abel after God accepted Abel's offering but not Cain's (Genesis 4: 1–10)

Dives and Lazarus—not the Lazarus who was raised from the dead in the New Testament, but a leprous beggar who was sent to heaven while a rich man, Dives, was sent to hell (Luke 16: 19–31)

baited bear—a bear that has been tied to a post and beaten or attacked by dogs or other animals for the sake of entertainment

O Ile leape …—the cry of Dr. Faustus, at the end of Christopher Marlowe's play of the same name, when he realizes he is damned because he made a pact with the devil in exchange for power and knowledge

laurel crown—a crown of victory

Aubade

Jane, Jane
Tall as a crane,
The morning light creaks down again;

Comb your cockscomb-ragged hair,
Jane, Jane come down the stair.

Each dull blunt wooden stalactite
Of rain creaks, hardened by the light,

Sounding like an overtone
From some lonely world unknown.

But the creaking empty light
Will never harden into sight,

Will never penetrate your brain
With overtones like the blunt rain.

The light would show (if it could harden)
Eternities of kitchen garden,

Cockscomb flowers that none will pluck,
And wooden flowers that 'gin to cluck.

In the kitchen you must light
Flames as staring, red and white,

As carrots or as turnips, shining
Where the cold dawn light lies whining.

Cockscomb hair on the cold wind.
Hangs limp, turns the milk's weak wind …

Jane, Jane
Tall as a crane,
The morning light creaks down again!

'gin—begin

Discussion Questions

1. An aubade is a poem about lovers who are forced to part in the morning. Traditionally, these are tender poems in which one lover tries to convince the other to stay. How does Sitwell play with this tradition, and to what effect?

2. What kind of person is Jane? What language suggests this?

FACTS

Symbolism

Symbolism was a movement in poetry and the arts that began in nineteenth-century France. It was an offshoot of the romantic movement, and the main thesis of the movement was that objects and images had specific symbolic meanings that could help the artist better portray the spiritual world. Often a system of symbolic elements would correspond to an emotion or feeling, and formal poetic structure was considered less important than the expression of these emotions or feelings. Major French symbolist poets include Charles Baudelaire (*Fleurs du mal*), Arthur Rimbaud, Stephane Mallarme, Paul Verlaine, and Paul Valery. These poets had a great influence on writers throughout Europe and America, especially writers like Ezra Pound, Dylan Thomas, H. D., E. E. Cummings, and Edith Sitwell.

Sir Beelzebub

When
Sir
Beelzebub called for his syllabub in the hotel in Hell
Where Proserpine first fell,
Blue as the gendarmerie were the waves of the sea,
(Rocking and shocking the bar-maid).
Nobody comes to give him his rum but the
Rim of the sky hippopotamus-glum
Enhances the chances to bless with a benison
Alfred Lord Tennyson crossing the bar laid
With cold vegetation from pale deputations
Of temperance workers (all signed In Memoriam)
Hoping with glory to trip up the Laureate's feet,

(Moving in classical metres) …
Like Balaclava, the lava came down from the
Roof, and the sea's blue wooden gendarmerie
Took them in charge while Beelzebub roared for his
rum.

… None of them come!

Beelzebub—a name for a demon or devil

syllabub—a drink made of milk or cream that is sweetened and mixed with wine

Proserpine—the Roman name for the Greek goddess Persephone, who was the goddess of spring. Pluto, the god of the Underworld, kidnapped Proserpine to be his bride. Her mother, Ceres, the goddess of the earth, was distraught, and everything on Earth stopped growing, causing winter. Eventually, Proserpine was allowed to visit her mother for a portion of the year (spring and summer) but she had to return to the Underworld each year to spend time with Pluto (fall and winter).

gendarmerie—soldiers or police officers

benison—a blessing spoken out loud

deputations—individuals who are authorized to speak on another's behalf

In Memoriam—Tennyson's elegy to his friend Arthur Hallam

Balaclava—a close-fitting hood or hat. Also the name of the part of the Crimea where the British Light Brigade was defeated. Tennyson's "The Charge of the Light Brigade" was one of his most famous poems.

Discussion Questions

1. How is Tennyson put into opposition with "Sir Beelzebub," and to what effect?

2. This poem was originally part of Sitwell's collection called *Façade,* in which she explored nonsense rhymes and unusual rhythms, among other things. What are some examples of the nonsense rhymes in this poem? How does this "nonsense" affect a reading of the poem?

Read More

Pearson, John. *The Sitwells: A Family's Biography.* New York: Harcourt Brace Jovanovich, 1980.

Sitwell, Edith. *Taken Care of: The Autobiography of Edith Sitwell.* New York: Atheneum, 1965.

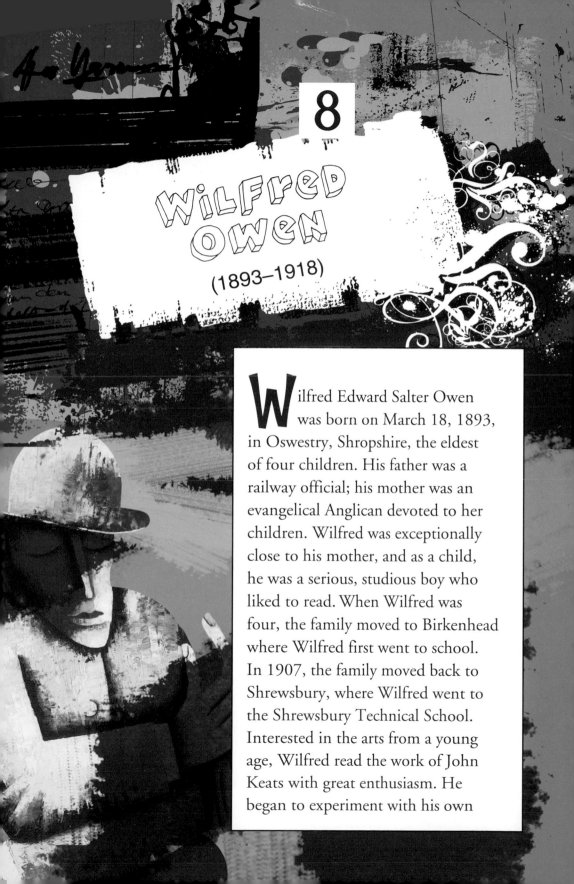

8

WiLFReD OWeN
(1893–1918)

Wilfred Edward Salter Owen was born on March 18, 1893, in Oswestry, Shropshire, the eldest of four children. His father was a railway official; his mother was an evangelical Anglican devoted to her children. Wilfred was exceptionally close to his mother, and as a child, he was a serious, studious boy who liked to read. When Wilfred was four, the family moved to Birkenhead where Wilfred first went to school. In 1907, the family moved back to Shrewsbury, where Wilfred went to the Shrewsbury Technical School. Interested in the arts from a young age, Wilfred read the work of John Keats with great enthusiasm. He began to experiment with his own

Wilfred Owen

poetry at age seventeen. After finishing school, Wilfred was unable to get a scholarship to attend University of London. Instead, he became a lay assistant to Reverend Herbert Wigan, for whom he worked for one year. In 1913, Owen moved to Bordeaux, France, where he began teaching English at the Berlitz School. After a year at the Berlitz, Owen began working as a private tutor for a French family. He was with them when World War I broke out.

Owen did not rush to the front, and his interest in the war grew relatively slowly. However, by September 1915, his interest had grown so strong that he enlisted in the Artists' Rifles, a group made up primarily of volunteers (though, actually, not many artists). Owen was commissioned as a second lieutenant in the Manchester Regiment and sent to France in 1916. Like many young men caught up in the patriotic fervor of the war, Owen was excited before going to the front. As he wrote to his mother, "There is a fine heroic feeling about being in France, and I am in perfect spirits."[1] After being at the front, however, his feelings took a dramatic turn: "I can see no excuse for deceiving you about these last 4 days. I have suffered seventh hell. I have not been at the front. I have been in front of it."[2]

After a several months of heart-wrenching battle, Owen was finally diagnosed as suffering from shell shock. Symptoms of shell shock, or "combat stress reaction" (CSR) as it is known today, include fatigue, slower reaction times, difficulty with prioritizing or completing tasks, and various physical ailments, such as tremors, headaches, and dizziness. After his diagnosis, Owen was sent to Craiglockhart War Hospital in Edinburgh. While in the hospital, Owen met Arthur Brock, a medical officer who, according to the BBC, "encouraged Owen to face the 'phantoms of the mind' and even exploit them in his poetry."[3] Owen also met the poet Siegfried Sassoon, whose work Owen greatly admired. During his recuperation, which he spent in Scotland, Owen met several of the country's notable literary figures through Sassoon, including Robert Graves, Sacheverell and Osbert Sitwell (the brothers of Edith Sitwell), and H. G. Wells.

Although he could have stayed in England, Owen felt compelled to return to the front to be near his fellow soldiers.[4] Owen went back to his regiment at the front in the summer of 1918. He was awarded the Military Cross for bravery for his actions at Amiens in October. Owen was killed by machine-gun fire on November 4, 1918, at Ors, just days before the end of the war. He was only twenty-five years old. His parents received word of his death on November 11, which was Armistice Day.

Two years later in 1920, *The Poems of Wilfred Owen* was published with an introduction by Sassoon. The work was immediately recognized as a poignant and telling depiction of the war, and it spoke to and inspired many artists. One of the most famous examples of this inspiration is composer Benjamin Britten's 1962 *War Requiem,* which continued to solidify Owen's place as one of the century's most important, if short-lived, poets. The *War Requiem* is a choral and orchestral funeral composition, which intersperses Owen's poems with more traditional Latin texts. Even today, Owen is considered to be one of the most influential war poets. According to one British veteran of the Iraq war: "Owen is the soldier's poet, because he understands what soldiering is really like, the horror and fear, alongside the dry-throated heroism."[5]

Dulce et Decorum Est

Bent double, like old beggars under sacks,
Knock-kneed, coughing like hags, we cursed through sludge,
Till on the haunting flares we turned our backs
And towards our distant rest began to trudge.
Men marched asleep. Many had lost their boots
But limped on, blood-shod. All went lame; all blind;
Drunk with fatigue; deaf even to the hoots
Of tired, outstripped Five-Nines that dropped behind.

Gas! Gas! Quick, boys!—An ecstasy of fumbling,
Fitting the clumsy helmets just in time;
But someone still was yelling out and stumbling
And flound'ring like a man in fire or lime...
Dim, through the misty panes and thick green light,
As under a green sea, I saw him drowning.

In all my dreams, before my helpless sight,
He plunges at me, guttering, choking, drowning.

If in some smothering dreams you too could pace
Behind the wagon that we flung him in,
And watch the white eyes writhing in his face,
His hanging face, like a devil's sick of sin;
If you could hear, at every jolt, the blood
Come gargling from the froth-corrupted lungs,
Obscene as cancer, bitter as the cud
Of vile, incurable sores on innocent tongues, —
My friend, you would not tell with such high zest
To children ardent for some desperate glory,
The old Lie: Dulce et decorum est
Pro patria mori.

Five-Nines—5.9-inch caliber shells

panes—windows of the gas mask

Anthem for Doomed Youth

What passing-bells for these who die as cattle?
Only the monstrous anger of the guns.
Only the stuttering rifles' rapid rattle
Can patter out their hasty orisons.
No mockeries now for them; no prayers nor bells;
Nor any voice of mourning save the choirs,
The shrill, demented choirs of wailing shells;
And bugles calling for them from sad shires.

What candles may be held to speed them all?
Not in the hands of boys, but in their eyes
Shall shine the holy glimmers of good-byes.
The pallor of girls' brows shall be their pall;
Their flowers the tenderness of patient minds,
And each slow dusk a drawing-down of blinds.

orisons—prayers

shires—counties

pall—a cloth that is laid over a coffin

Discussion Questions

1. Does this poem correspond to your understanding of an anthem? Why or why not?

2. What does this poem suggest about funerals and death ceremonies in battle? What language suggests this?

3. How do the descriptions of sound change as the poem progresses?

This posed photo, taken in France near the front-line trenches, was staged to show the effects of phosgene gas on troops.

Exposure

Our brains ache, in the merciless iced east winds that knive us...
Wearied we keep awake because the night is silent...
Low, drooping flares confuse our memory of the salient ...
Worried by silence, sentries whisper, curious, nervous,
But nothing happens.
Watching, we hear the mad gusts tugging on the wire,
Like twitching agonies of men among its brambles.
Northward, incessantly, the flickering gunnery rumbles,
Far off, like a dull rumour of some other war.
What are we doing here?

The poignant misery of dawn begins to grow...
We only know war lasts, rain soaks, and clouds sag stormy.
Dawn massing in the east her melancholy army
Attacks once more in ranks on shivering of grey,
But nothing happens.

Sudden successive flights of bullets streak the silence.
Less deathly than the air that shudders black with snow,
With sidelong flowing flakes that flock, pause, and renew;
We watch them wandering up and down the wind's nonchalance,
But nothing happens.

Pale flakes with fingering stealth come feeling for our faces -
We cringe in holes, back on forgotten dreams, and stare, snow-dazed,
Deep into grassier ditches. So we drowse, sun-dozed,
Littered with blossoms trickling where the blackbird fusses,
Is it that we are dying?

Slowly our ghosts drag home: glimpsing the sunk fires, glozed
With crusted dark-red jewels; crickets jingle there;
For hours the innocent mice rejoice: the house is theirs;
Shutters and doors, all closed: on us the doors are closed, -
We turn back to our dying.

Since we believe not otherwise can kind fires burn;
Nor ever suns smile true on child, or field, or fruit.
For God's invincible spring our love is made afraid;
Therefore, not loath, we lie out here; therefore were born,
For love of God seems dying.

To-night, this frost will fasten on this mud and us,
Shrivelling many hands, puckering foreheads crisp.
The burying-party, picks and shovels in shaking grasp,
Pause over half-known faces. All their eyes are ice,
But nothing happens.

salient—a position on the front that jutted out into enemy territory

grey—the color of the German uniforms

glozed—glossed

Discussion Questions

1. What is the structure of this poem? How does the structure of the poem reinforce the theme of the pointlessness of war?

2. How is nature imagery used in this poem?

3. The poem repeatedly says that "nothing happens." Is this accurate? Why or why not?

4. Imperfect rhyme is deliberately partial, or "near," rhyme in which the rhyme between vowels is approximate only. How is imperfect rhyme used in this poem and to what effect?

Read More

Stallworthy, Jon. *Wilfred Owen.* New York: Oxford University Press, 1993.

Walter, George, ed. *The Penguin Book of First World War Poetry.* New York: Penguin Classics, 2007.

Stevie Smith

(1902–1971)

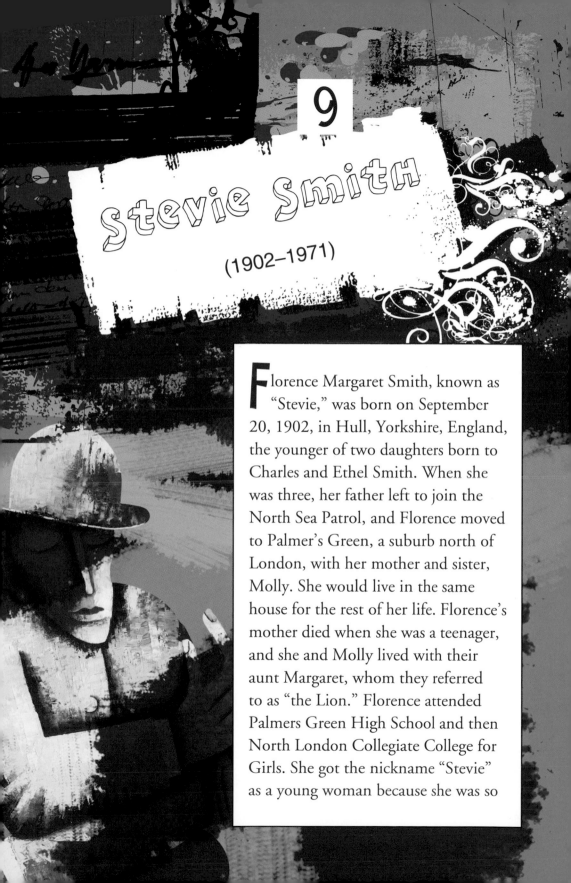

Florence Margaret Smith, known as "Stevie," was born on September 20, 1902, in Hull, Yorkshire, England, the younger of two daughters born to Charles and Ethel Smith. When she was three, her father left to join the North Sea Patrol, and Florence moved to Palmer's Green, a suburb north of London, with her mother and sister, Molly. She would live in the same house for the rest of her life. Florence's mother died when she was a teenager, and she and Molly lived with their aunt Margaret, whom they referred to as "the Lion." Florence attended Palmers Green High School and then North London Collegiate College for Girls. She got the nickname "Stevie" as a young woman because she was so

Stevie Smith

petite that she reminded friends of a famous jockey of the time named Steve Donoghue.[1]

After finishing school, Smith became the secretary for George Newnes, Sir Neville Pearson, and Sir Frank Newnes at Newnes Publishing Company. While working there, Smith began to write seriously. Her work was influenced by her reading of Tennyson and Browning and by everyday events. She did not, however, often read the work of her contemporaries. By the 1930s, Smith was writing prolifically, but it was not until 1936 that some of her poems were published in the liberal magazine *New Statesman.* The initial response to these poems was positive, and in the next two years, two collections of her poems were published by Jonathan Cape, including *A Good Time Was Had by All* (1937) and *Tender Only to One* (1938). These collections contained sketches and doodles that Smith had created to accompany the poems, which she would continue to do throughout her life. During her time as a secretary, Smith also wrote novels, including *A Novel on Yellow Paper* (1936), *Over the Frontier* (1938), and *The Holiday* (1949). Although fictional, Smith's novels often included autobiographical incidents and characters. Despite the success of her novels, Smith's writing focused mainly on poetry.

Although the tone of Smith's poems was light, almost like nursery rhymes, the subject matter was often very dark, focusing on such topics as death and loneliness. She was critical of snobbery and was socially liberal; her opinions, however, were generally played out in her poems, not in her actions. During World War II, Smith continued writing while she performed fire-watching duty, keeping an eye out for fires that started as a result of bombs dropped by the Germans. In 1942, her collection of poetry *Mother, What Is Man?* was published. Despite her rising fame and her circle of intellectual acquaintances, which included George Orwell, among others, Smith continued to live in her rather humble home in Palmer's Green with her aunt. In 1953, she retired from the publishing company to focus her energies on writing. In 1957, Smith published the collection *Not Waving but Drowning,* which included her most famous poem. After this collection was published, Smith's stature in literary circles was assured, but because her work was so unique, she was often overlooked by the public. In praising the 1957 collection, David Wright wrote:

> As one of the most original women poets now writing [Stevie Smith] seems to have missed most of the public accolades bestowed by critics and anthologists. One reason may be that not only does she belong to no "school"—whether real or invented as they usually are—but her work is so completely different from anyone else's that it is all but impossible to discuss her poems in relation to those of her contemporaries.[2]

FACTS

Wartime London

In late 1940 and early 1941, Germany systematically launched air attacks against Great Britain in an effort that became known as the Battle of Britain. The most intense bombing took place in September and October 1940. The blitzkrieg—or simply blitz—was particularly damaging in major cities like London, where more than a million homes were destroyed. Although the attacks were meant to demoralize the British populace, they were ultimately unsuccessful, although there were forty-three thousand civilian casualties. Throughout the war, civilians were forced to ration food and supplies, submit to blackouts, and flee to bomb shelters, especially in the cities where people used the subway or "Underground" stations to stay safe from the bombs. City children were sent to live in the countryside to escape the bombing, and gas masks were issued for everyone, including babies.

In the 1960s, Smith became a popular, if eccentric, figure at literary readings where she often half-sang her poems. During this time, she gained many admirers, including the poet Sylvia Plath. In 1963, Smith won the first Cholmondeley Award, the annual poetry award from the Society of Authors in the United Kingdom, and in 1969 she won the Queen's Gold Medal for Poetry.

Smith cared for her aging aunt until her aunt died in 1968 at the age of ninety-six. After "the Lion's" death, Smith became ill herself, and soon had trouble finding words. She was soon diagnosed with a brain tumor, and she died on March 7, 1971, in Devon, where her elder sister lived. After her death, Smith's poetry gained even more respect, and her *Collected Poems* was published in 1975. In 1977, playwright Hugh Whitemore wrote the play *Stevie,* which is based on Smith's life. This play was made into a film in 1978.

Not Waving but Drowning

*Nobody heard him, the dead man, But still he lay
moaning:
I was much further out than you thought
And not waving but drowning.*

*Poor chap, he always loved larking
And now he's dead
It must have been too cold for him his heart gave way,
They said.*

*Oh, no no no, it was too cold always
(Still the dead one lay moaning)
I was much too far out all my life
And not waving but drowning.*

Summary and Explication: "Not Waving but Drowning"

One of Smith's most famous poems, "Not Waving but Drowning" is part of a collection of the same name, which was praised as "the best collection of new poems to appear in 1957," according to *Poetry* contributor David Wright.[3] Smith was inspired to write this poem after reading an article about a man who drowned after his friends thought he was waving to them, not struggling, in the sea.[4]

The poem is an unsuccessful dialogue between the dead man and the people on the shore. In the first stanza, the dead man speaks, or moans, in a final attempt to communicate that he had not actually been waving. The second stanza is spoken by an individual who had failed to recognize his needs. Those on the shore knew the drowned man as one who loved larking—joking around and playing—throughout his life, and they assumed that he simply had a heart attack while continuing his fun. In the third stanza, the reader sees that the dead man was never able to communicate his true feelings, which were much "further out," and that he felt "too cold always," suggesting that although he may have seemed happy, he was always feeling despair.

Techniques and Devices

Free verse is verse that is printed in short lines but without any organized meter or rhyme scheme. "Not Waving but Drowning" is written in free verse that mirrors a dialogue between the drowning man and those on the shore.

Interpretation

"Not Waving but Drowning" offers a poignant message about failed communication among individuals and in society in general. In this

British actress Glenda Jackson played the title role in the play *Stevie*, based on the life of Stevie Smith.

poem, there is a dialogue of missed cues between the drowned man and society, as it is represented by his friends on the shore. While the story is about the moment of his death in the water, the missed signals seem to have existed during the moments leading up to his death and throughout his life: "it was too cold always." At the end of the poem, the response of the man's friends, or society in general, is not shown, which offers another indication that the conversation failed before it even began.

Discussion Questions

1. How does the lighthearted tone of this poem affect an understanding of the poem's theme of failed communication? Why?

2. What is the impact of the repetition of the line "And not waving but drowning"?

3. What does being "offshore," away from civilization, signal about the drowning man?

Tender Only to One

Tender only to one
Tender and true
The petals swing
To my fingering
Is it you, or you, or you?

Tender only to one
I do not know his name
And the friends who fall
To the petals' call
May think my love to blame.

Tender only to one
This petal holds a clue
The face it shows
But too well knows
Who I am tender to.

Tender only to one,
Last petal's latest breath
Cries out aloud
From the icy shroud
His name, his name is Death.

Discussion Questions

1. What is the impact of using the simple child's game of picking petals off a flower as a means of illustrating the finality—and certainty—of death?

2. Do you think that Death is a negative character here? Why or why not?

3. What is the rhyme scheme of this poem? What is the impact of the repetition of "Tender only to one"?

Read More

Huk, Romana. *Stevie Smith: Between the Lines.* New York: Palgrave Macmillan, 2005.

Spalding, Frances. *Stevie Smith: A Biography.* New York: W. W. Norton, 1989.

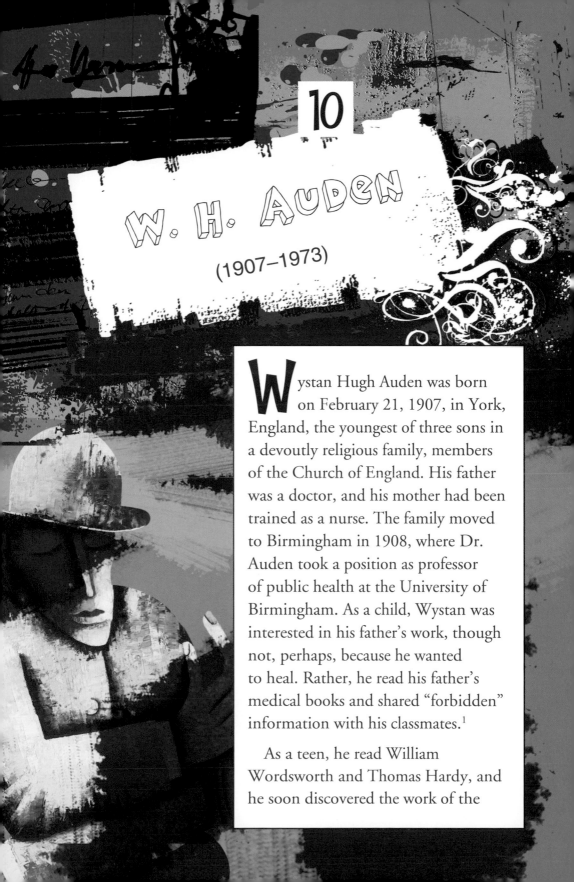

W. H. Auden

(1907–1973)

Wystan Hugh Auden was born on February 21, 1907, in York, England, the youngest of three sons in a devoutly religious family, members of the Church of England. His father was a doctor, and his mother had been trained as a nurse. The family moved to Birmingham in 1908, where Dr. Auden took a position as professor of public health at the University of Birmingham. As a child, Wystan was interested in his father's work, though not, perhaps, because he wanted to heal. Rather, he read his father's medical books and shared "forbidden" information with his classmates.[1]

As a teen, he read William Wordsworth and Thomas Hardy, and he soon discovered the work of the

A painting of W. H. Auden by Jeffrey Morgan

American poet T. S. Eliot. While at school, Auden was already a prolific writer, and some of his poems were published in the school magazine. He attended Christ Church College at Oxford, where he continued to write, although he ultimately graduated with poor marks. While at the university, Auden met Cecil Day Lewis, who eventually became poet laureate of England; Stephen Spender, who became a poet and novelist; and Christopher Isherwood, whom Auden had met in childhood and who would become an important novelist and playwright. Auden and Isherwood were both homosexual, and Isherwood had a great influence on Auden, especially in terms of his literary career. The two remained friends and collaborators for much of their lives. After graduating, Auden traveled to Berlin for a year, where he took advantage of the sexually tolerant atmosphere. After about nine months, he returned to England, where he taught at various prep schools while continuing to write.

Auden's first major collection, *Poems,* was published in 1930 by T. S. Eliot, who was an editor at Faber and Faber at the time. The book was well received. In the 1930s, Auden traveled extensively and was soon well regarded as a poet, albeit a politically liberal one. According to his literary executor, Edward Mendelson, "No English poet since Byron achieved fame so quickly."[2] In his lifetime, Auden published several dozen collections, including a few that included revisions of previously published work. As Mendelson later recalled, "In revising his poems, Auden opened his workshop to the public, and the spectacle proved unsettling, especially as his revisions … moved against the current of literary fashion."[3] Throughout his life, Auden also worked in a variety of forms other than poetry. For example, as a young man, he worked on a documentary called *Night Mail* (1936) for the General Post Office's Film Unit. Through this project, he met composer Benjamin Britten, with whom he would collaborate as a lyricist on later projects. He collaborated on three plays with his friend Isherwood. He also wrote the lyrics for several operas, including Igor Stravinsky's *The Rake's Progress.*

In 1935, Auden married Erika Mann, the daughter of the German novelist, so that she could escape Nazi Germany. This was a marriage of convenience, and it was never consummated.[4] In 1937, Auden went to Spain, where he worked briefly as a radio broadcaster in the Spanish Civil War. After this experience, he wrote a long political poem, "Spain," in support of the Spanish Republican cause. In 1938, Auden also traveled to China with Isherwood to report on the Sino-Japanese War, and together, they wrote *Journey to a War,*

FACTS

The Spanish Civil War

The Spanish Civil War took place from 1936 to 1939, the period directly preceding World War II. The war began when a group tried to overthrow the newly elected government. This group was known as the nationalists and was led by General Francisco Franco. Individuals who sided with the newly elected government were known as loyalists or republicans. In general, the loyalists—many of whom were socialists or even communists—received support from the Soviet Union and other socialist or communist countries. The nationalists received support from Germany and Italy, which were led by fascist dictators at the time. Many American and British citizens were drawn to this conflict on the side of the loyalists, including W. H. Auden and Ernest Hemingway.

which was published in 1939. After their trip to China, Auden and Isherwood traveled to the United States, and they decided to move there permanently the following year. Isherwood eventually went to California, while Auden stayed in New York, although the pair remained friends. In New York, Auden met Chester Kallman, a young Brooklynite, and fell in love. Their occasionally turbulent relationship lasted for the rest of Auden's life. During this time, Auden also began attending services in the Episcopal Church, a practice he had abandoned as a young teenager. He wrote and taught at various universities, including the University of Michigan and Swarthmore, among others. Auden became an American citizen in 1946.

According to a letter to his friend Peggy Garland, Auden hated New York's hot summers.[5] In 1948, Auden rented a summer home in Italy. Thereafter, Auden spent his summers in Europe, first in Italy, and then in Austria, where he eventually purchased a home in Kirchstetten. From 1956 to 1961, he was a professor of poetry at Oxford University, though he only had to give a few lectures a year. From 1954 to his death, he was a chancellor of the Academy of American Poets. In the last year of his life, Auden was offered a cottage at Oxford University, which he accepted. On September 28, 1973, after having given a poetry reading in Vienna, he had a heart attack and died. He is buried in Kirchstetten and is memorialized with a plaque in Poets' Corner in Westminster Abbey.

Musée des Beaux Arts

About suffering they were never wrong,
The Old Masters; how well they understood
Its human position; how it takes place
While someone else is eating or opening a window or just
walking dully along;
How, when the aged are reverently, passionately waiting
For the miraculous birth, there always must be
Children who did not specially want it to happen, skating
On a pond at the edge of the wood:
They never forgot
That even the dreadful martyrdom must run its course
Anyhow in a corner, some untidy spot
Where the dogs go on with their doggy
life and the torturer's horse
Scratches its innocent behind on a tree.

In Brueghel's Icarus, for instance: how everything turns away
Quite leisurely from the disaster; the ploughman may
Have heard the splash, the forsaken cry,
But for him it was not an important failure; the sun shone
As it had to on the white legs disappearing into the green
Water; and the expensive delicate ship that must have seen
Something amazing, a boy falling out of the sky,
Had somewhere to get to and sailed calmly on.

Old Masters—master painters, or the paintings that they created

miraculous birth—that of Jesus

Summary and Explication : "Musée des Beaux Arts"

The title "Musée des Beaux Arts" is French for "Museum of Fine Art," which establishes the setting for the poem as a museum. The first stanza references the "old masters," who were artists who created masterpieces and who seemed, according to the speaker, to be so observant that they could see and depict the "human position" of suffering—or rather, how one person's suffering relates to the rest of the world, a world in which other people are doing everyday things like eating, walking, or even simply opening a window. The speaker then references the "miraculous birth" or the birth of Jesus, and points out that the "old masters" were apt to paint the scene with children playing in the background, unaware of the miracle going on right near them. Similarly, they would paint the "martyrdom," or Jesus's death, and the paintings would include images of Jesus's suffering alongside an image of a dog or a horse who is, of course, oblivious to the drama.

In the second stanza, the speaker references a famous painting by Pieter Brueghel, a sixteenth-century Flemish painter known for painting landscapes and peasant scenes. In this painting, which is actually entitled Landscape with the Fall of Icarus, Brueghel painted a seemingly peaceful landscape. In the painting, a farmer is working with a plough in the field, and a ship with a tall mast is sailing purposefully along in the background. In the midst of this calm, however, is the fall of Icarus, a dramatic and tragic event described in a Greek myth. In that story, Icarus and his father, Daedalus, had made wings out of wax. Before they took off, Daedalus warned Icarus not to fly too high or the sun would melt the wax and he would fall. Icarus loved flying so much that he did, indeed, fly too high. The sun melted the wax of his wings, and he fell to his death. In Brueghel's painting, the tragedy happens and though the situation would have seemed all-consuming to Daedalus, the other characters in the painting hardly notice.

Interpretation

In "Musée des Beaux Arts," Auden refers to Brueghel's painting to show that in reality, good and bad events do not happen in a vacuum. Rather, if and when momentous events do occur, everyday events continue on as well. By referencing a painting in which life continues to go on despite the dramatic death of a young man, the poem illustrates the vastness of the human condition at the same time as it highlights the apathy that some individuals have toward those in need.

Discussion Questions

1. Breugel's painting *Landscape with the Fall of Icarus* is a seemingly peaceful landscape/harbor scene. Only Icarus's legs can be seen flailing in the water. How does this tragedy fit in with such a peaceful scene?

2. What other comparative images can be found in the poem?

3. "Musée des Beaux Arts" was written in December 1938 and published in 1940. Does this fact influence your reading of the poem? Why or why not?

The Unknown Citizen

(To JS/07 M 378
This Marble Monument Is Erected by the State)

He was found by the Bureau of Statistics to be
One against whom there was no official complaint,
And all the reports on his conduct agree
That, in the modern sense of an old-fashioned word, he was a saint,
For in everything he did he served the Greater Community.
Except for the War till the day he retired
He worked in a factory and never got fired,
But satisfied his employers, Fudge Motors Inc.
Yet he wasn't a scab or odd in his views,
For his Union reports that he paid his dues,
(Our report on his Union shows it was sound)
And our Social Psychology workers found
That he was popular with his mates and liked a drink.
The Press are convinced that he bought a paper every day
And that his reactions to advertisements were normal in every way.
Policies taken out in his name prove that he was fully insured,
And his Health-card shows he was once in hospital but left it cured.
Both Producers Research and High-Grade Living declare
He was fully sensible to the advantages of the Installment Plan
And had everything necessary to the Modern Man,
A phonograph, a radio, a car and a frigidaire.
Our researchers into Public Opinion are content
That he held the proper opinions for the time of year;

When there was peace, he was for peace: when there was war, he went.
He was married and added five children to the population,
Which our Eugenist says was the right number for a parent of his generation.
And our teachers report that he never interfered with their education.
Was he free? Was he happy? The question is absurd:
Had anything been wrong, we should certainly have heard.

scab—a worker who refuses to participate in a labor union's strike; someone who takes a striking worker's job

Eugenist—someone who studies the possibility of improving human populations

Discussion Questions

1. What kind of person was the unknown citizen? Can you tell, and if so, how? If not, why not?

2. What kind of society did the unknown citizen live in, and what language makes you think so? What kind of statement does this poem make about a society that would respond to a man's death in this way?

3. What is the effect of the closing couplet?

Auden (on right) with fellow British writer Christopher Isherwood

In Memory of W. B. Yeats

I

He disappeared in the dead of winter:
The brooks were frozen, the airports almost deserted,
And snow disfigured the public statues;
The mercury sank in the mouth of the dying day.
O all instruments we have agree
The day of his death was a dark cold day.

Far from his illness
The wolves ran on through the evergreen forests,
The peasant river was untempted by the fashionable quays;
By mourning tongues
The death of the poet was kept from his poems.

III

Earth, receive an honoured guest:
William Yeats is laid to rest.
Let the Irish vessel lie
Emptied of its poetry.

In the nightmare of the dark
All the dogs of Europe bark,
And the living nations wait,
Each sequestered in its hate;

Intellectual disgrace
Stares from every human face,
And the seas of pity lie
Locked and frozen in each eye.

Follow, poet, follow right
To the bottom of the night,
With your unconstraining voice
Still persuade us to rejoice;

With the farming of a verse
Make a vineyard of the curse,
Sing of human unsuccess
In a rapture of distress;

In the deserts of the heart
Let the healing fountain start,
In the prison of his days
Teach the free man how to praise.

quays—wharves

Discussion Questions

1. The poet W. B. Yeats died January 29, 1939, in southern France. This poem was written in February 1939 and published in 1940. Although this is an elegy, does the speaker admire Yeats unconditionally? Why or why not?

2. How does this poem suggest that Yeats will live on after death?

3. World War II did not officially begin until September 1939. How does World War II loom over this poem and over the memory of Yeats? What language suggests this?

4. The third section of the poem has a very regular rhythm and rhyme scheme, unlike the rest of the poem. What impact does this have? How does the structure of each section correspond to the theme or focus of that section?

Read More

Smith, Stan, ed. *The Cabridge Companion to W. H. Auden.* Cambridge: Cambridge University Press, 2005.

Spears, Monroe K. *The Poetry of W. H. Auden: The Disenchanted Island.* New York: Oxford University Press, 1963.

DYLAN THOMAS

(1914–1953)

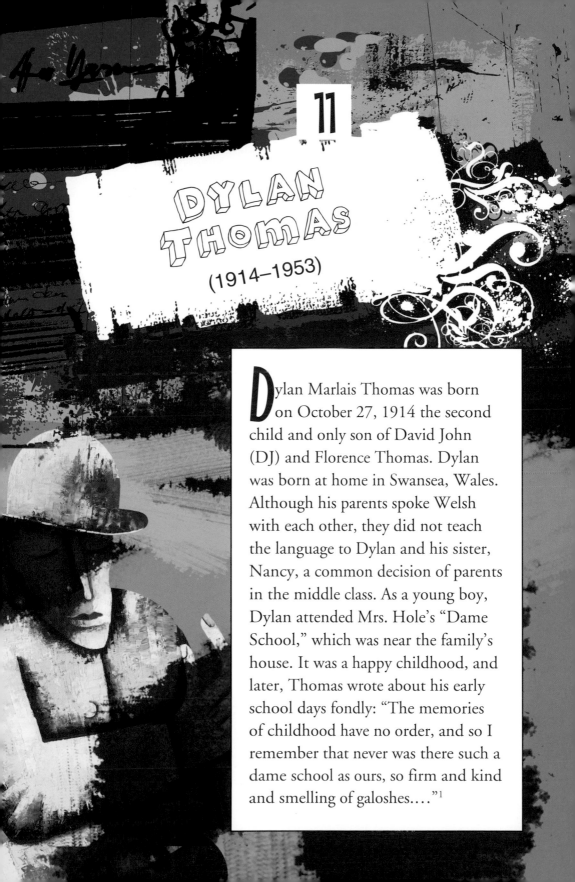

Dylan Marlais Thomas was born on October 27, 1914 the second child and only son of David John (DJ) and Florence Thomas. Dylan was born at home in Swansea, Wales. Although his parents spoke Welsh with each other, they did not teach the language to Dylan and his sister, Nancy, a common decision of parents in the middle class. As a young boy, Dylan attended Mrs. Hole's "Dame School," which was near the family's house. It was a happy childhood, and later, Thomas wrote about his early school days fondly: "The memories of childhood have no order, and so I remember that never was there such a dame school as ours, so firm and kind and smelling of galoshes...."[1]

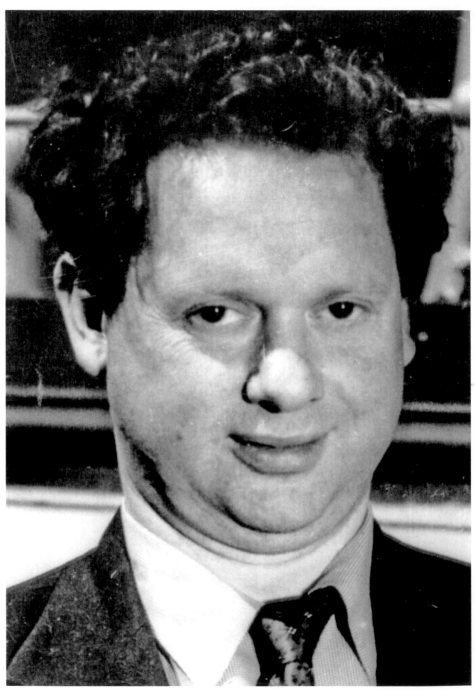

Dylan Thomas

In 1925, Dylan began attending the Swansea Grammar School, where his father was a schoolmaster who taught literature and who was in charge of the school magazine. Dylan immediately submitted poems to the school magazine, and soon it was regularly publishing his work. He was an unruly student, however, and the only subject that he did well in was English. Dylan left school in 1931 at the age of sixteen to become a journalist at the *South Wales Daily Post,* where he worked for a little more than a year. During this time, Dylan joined the Swansea Little Theatre Company, which was located in Mumbles. He acted in several plays, as did his sister and several of their friends.

At the age of eighteen, Thomas decided to dedicate himself to working full-time on his poetry. A year later, his poem "And Death Shall Have No Dominion" was published in the *New English Weekly.* It was his first poem to be published outside of school, and the first of his poems to be published outside of Wales. That year, Thomas traveled to London for the first time, where he stayed with his sister, who had moved to London after her marriage. In 1934, Thomas moved to London, where he shared an apartment with two Swansea-born artists, Alfred James and Mervyn Levy. During this time, he developed a reputation as a heavy drinker, a habit that would continue throughout his life. In late 1934, Thomas won the Poets' Corner prize, sponsored by the *Sunday Referee,* a newspaper. Part of the award was a sponsorship to publish his first book, *18 Poems.* The collection did not sell particularly well, but it received praise from several established poets, including Edith Sitwell.[2] Most of the poems in this collection had been written at his family's home in Swansea.

An attractive, deep-voiced man, Thomas questioned everything. Later, his long-time friend and correspondent Vernon Watkins described him on their first meeting in 1934:

He was slight, shorter than I had expected, shy, rather flushed and eager in manner, deep-voiced, restless, humorous, with large, wondering, yet acutely intelligent eyes, gold curls, snub nose, and the face of a cherub. I quickly realized when we went for a walk on the cliffs that this cherub took nothing for granted. In thought and words he was anarchic, challenging, with the certainty of that instinct which knows its own freshly discovered truth.[3]

In April 1936, Thomas met Caitlin Macnamara, an Irish dancer living in London. The pair fell in love, and they were married in 1937 in Cornwall. The couple's relationship was stormy, with affairs on both sides. They had three children: sons Llewelyn (1939–2000) and Colm (born 1949) and daughter Aeronwy (born 1943).

Always sickly, Thomas was declared medically unfit for military service during World War II. The family lived in London off

FACTS

Wales

Like Northern Ireland and Scotland, Wales is a country within the United Kingdom. Cardiff is the capital of Wales; Swansea and Newport are two other major urban areas. Today, both English and Welsh, a Celtic language, are spoken throughout the country. Renewed interest in the Welsh national tradition developed in the early twentieth century and continues today. Literature and music, especially poetry and singing, are celebrated in Wales, and the country is often referred to as the "Land of Song."

and on during the war, though they moved frequently and left during the worst of the air raids. Thomas wrote scenarios for war documentaries, and eventually began broadcasting on BBC radio programs, an activity he would continue regularly until his death.

After the war, Thomas and his family eventually settled in Laugharne, Wales, but Thomas began to travel abroad regularly. In 1947, he received a travel scholarship from the Society of Authors to visit Italy. In 1949, he visited Prague, and in 1950, he traveled to America for a vast—and hugely successful—reading tour across the United States and Canada. In 1951, he traveled to Persia (now Iran) as a scriptwriter for the Anglo-Iranian Oil Company. From 1952 to 1953, he returned to the United States three more times.

After more than two decades of hard drinking, Thomas became seriously ill during his fourth visit to the United States in 1953, where he had gone for the premiere of his play *Under Milk Wood*. On November 5, 1953, he collapsed at the Chelsea Hotel in New York City. He died four days later on November 9, 1953, at St. Vincent's Hospital at the age of thirty-nine. His body was transported back to Wales where he was buried in Laugharne on November 25, 1953. Thomas is recognized today by a plaque in Westminster Abbey.

Do Not Go Gentle into That Good Night

Do not go gentle into that good night,
Old age should burn and rave at close of day;
Rage, rage against the dying of the light.

Though wise men at their end know dark is right,
Because their words had forked no lightning they
Do not go gentle into that good night.

Good men, the last wave by, crying how bright
Their frail deeds might have danced in a green bay,
Rage, rage against the dying of the light.

Wild men who caught and sang the sun in flight,
And learn, too late, they grieved it on its way,
Do not go gentle into that good night.

Grave men, near death, who see with blinding sight
Blind eyes could blaze like meteors and be gay,
Rage, rage against the dying of the light.

And you, my father, there on the sad height,
Curse, bless, me now with your fierce tears, I pray,
Do not go gentle into that good night.
Rage, rage against the dying of the light.

rave—to talk wildly

Summary and Explication: "Do Not Go Gentle into That Good Night"

"Do Not Go Gentle into That Good Night" is one of Dylan Thomas's most famous and most often quoted poems. It was written during the end of Thomas's father's life, though the speaker is not necessarily Thomas speaking to his father on his deathbed.

By suggesting that he "not go gentle" into "that good night," or death, the speaker is urging his father to live his life to the end. He offers evidence of how—despite death's inevitability—different men refused to acquiesce to it. In the first stanza, the speaker offers the idea that in old age, men often "burn and rave" as they get closer to death. In the second stanza, in the face of death, wise men learn that their bright words cannot compete with lightning. In the third stanza, good men at the "last wave" come to understand that their deeds are nothing compared to the calm bay. In the fourth stanza, wild men learn that they cannot stop the sun from setting. In the fifth stanza, grave men accept happiness as death approaches. The final stanza begs the father to act, to "rage," to live his life to the fullest until its final day. The somewhat paradoxical message is that death cannot be overcome—yet we must fight it.

Techniques and Devices

"Do Not Go Gentle into That Good Night" is a villanelle, a strictly formatted poem that consists of five three-line stanzas, or tercets, and one four-line stanza, or quatrain. A villanelle has only two rhyme sounds (here, the rhyme sounds are *-ight* and *-ay*). Finally, the first and last lines of the first stanza are repeated alternately in each of the following stanzas until the final stanza, where they form a couplet to close the poem.

Interpretation

With the repeated emphasis to "Rage, rage against the dying of the light," this poem seems to suggest that the speaker is admonishing his father to fight death. However, the comparisons within the poem recognize that death is inevitable and that men must come to accept this. In light of these comparisons, the speaker seems to be admonishing his father to not give up and fall away from his true "fierce" character, for it will only be in this way that he will be able to come to an acceptance of death as part of the natural order.

Discussion Questions

1. What nature images are used to portray death in this poem, and to what effect?

2. The villanelle format requires complete control and, to some degree, conformity. What is the effect, then, of the repeated use of the word "rage" throughout this poem?

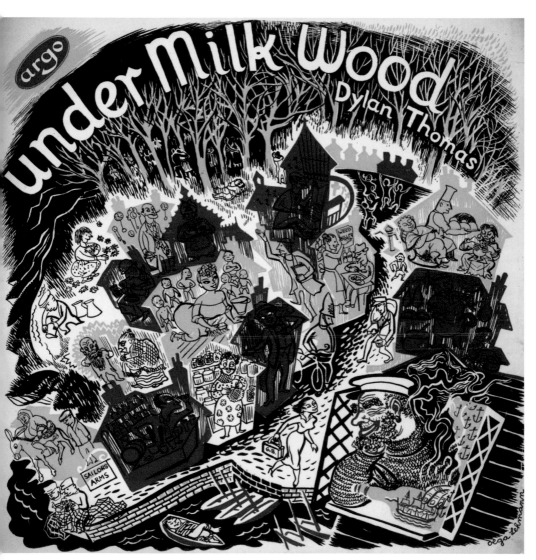

The book cover for Thomas's play *Under Milk Wood*. In both his poetry and his prose, Dylan Thomas drew on his Welsh childhood.

Fern Hill

Now as I was young and easy under the apple boughs
About the lilting house and happy as the grass was green,
The night above the dingle starry,
Time let me hail and climb
Golden in the heydays of his eyes,
And honoured among wagons I was prince of the apple towns
And once below a time I lordly had the trees and leaves
Trail with daisies and barley
Down the rivers of the windfall light.

And as I was green and carefree, famous among the barns
About the happy yard and singing as the farm was home,
In the sun that is young once only,
Time let me play and be
Golden in the mercy of his means,
And green and golden I was huntsman and herdsman, the calves
Sang to my horn, the foxes on the hills barked clear and cold,
And the sabbath rang slowly
In the pebbles of the holy streams.

All the sun long it was running, it was lovely, the hay
Fields high as the house, the tunes from the chimneys, it was air
And playing, lovely and watery
And fire green as grass.
And nightly under the simple stars
As I rode to sleep the owls were bearing the farm away,
All the moon long I heard, blessed among stables, the nightjars
Flying with the ricks, and the horses
Flashing into the dark.

And then to awake, and the farm, like a wanderer white
With the dew, come back, the cock on his shoulder: it was all
Shining, it was Adam and maiden,
The sky gathered again
And the sun grew round that very day.
So it must have been after the birth of the simple light
In the first, spinning place, the spellbound horses walking warm
Out of the whinnying green stable
On to the fields of praise.

And honoured among foxes and pheasants by the gay house
Under the new made clouds and happy as the heart was long,
In the sun born over and over,
I ran my heedless ways,
My wishes raced through the house high hay
And nothing I cared, at my sky blue trades, that time allows
In all his tuneful turning so few and such morning songs
Before the children green and golden
Follow him out of grace.

Nothing I cared, in the lamb white days, that time would take me
Up to the swallow thronged loft by the shadow of my hand,
In the moon that is always rising,
Nor that riding to sleep
I should hear him fly with the high fields
And wake to the farm forever fled from the childless land.
Oh as I was young and easy in the mercy of his means,
Time held me green and dying
Though I sang in my chains like the sea.

dingle—a small wooded valley or dell

windfall—something that falls from the tree because of the wind, like fruit; a sudden good fortune

nightjars—birds that fly at night

ricks—stacks of hay

Discussion Questions

1. While the speaker is not necessarily Thomas, it is important to note that Fern Hill was the home of Thomas's aunt, where he spent his summers as a child. What language is used to idealize Fern Hill and the speaker's youth?

2. How is nature imagery used in this poem?

3. Does the tone of this poem change as it progresses? What is the meaning of the closing line?

4. Describe the structure of this poem. How do rhyme and meter give the poem an overall musical quality?

The Force That Through the Green Fuse Drives the Flower

The force that through the green fuse drives the flower
Drives my green age; that blasts the roots of trees
Is my destroyer.
And I am dumb to tell the crooked rose
My youth is bent by the same wintry fever.

The force that drives the water through the rocks
Drives my red blood; that dries the mouthing streams
Turns mine to wax.
And I am dumb to mouth unto my veins
How at the mountain spring the same mouth sucks.

The hand that whirls the water in the pool
Stirs the quicksand; that ropes the blowing wind
Hauls my shroud sail.
And I am dumb to tell the hanging man
How of my clay is made the hangman's lime

The lips of time leech to the fountain head;
Love drips and gathers, but the fallen blood
Shall calm her sores.
And I am dumb to tell a weather's wind
How time has ticked a heaven round the stars.

And I am dumb to tell the lover's tomb
How at my sheet goes the same crooked worm.

lime—quicklime, which would be poured over a grave to quicken
decomposition

leech—suck or fasten on

sheet—as in a shroud for a corpse

Discussion Questions

1. What is "the force"? How is it used to illustrate the cycle of life?

2. How is the nature imagery in this poem juxtaposed with death imagery?

Read More

Jones, Daniel, ed. *The Poems of Dylan Thomas.* New York: New Directions, 2003.

Thomas, Dylan (Chris Raschka, illustrator). *A Child's Christmas in Wales.* Cambridge, Mass.: Candlewick Press, 2004.

Introduction

1. Adapterd from Paula Johanson, *Early British Poetry:—"Words That Burn"* (Berkeley Hcights, N.J.: Enslow Publishers, Inc., 2010), p. 9.

2. Ibid.

Chapter 1. Elizabeth Barrett Browning

1. "Elizabeth Barrett Browning," The Academy of American Poets, 1997–2006, <http://www.poets.org/poet.php/prmPID/152> (March 30, 2008).

2. Sarah Knowles Bolton, *The Lives of Girls Who Became Famous,* 1914, Project Gutenberg, <http://www.gutenberg.org/ files/12081/12081-h/12081-h.htm#c12> (March 30, 2008).

3. Rosemary Sprague, *Forever in Joy: The Life of Robert Browning* (New York: Chilton Books, 1965), p. 60.

Chapter 2. Robert Browning

1. Rosemary Sprague, *Forever in Joy: The Life of Robert Browning* (New York: Chilton Books, 1965), p. 26.

2. Robert Browning, "Letter, January 10, 1845." Quoted in Angela Leighton and Margaret Reynolds, *Victorian Women Poets: An Anthology* (Cambridge, Mass.: Blackwell Publishers, 1995), p. 64.

3. Sprague, p. 154.

4. C. D. Merriman, "Robert Browning," The Literature Network, Jalic, Inc., 2006, <http://www.online-literature.com/robert-browning/> (March 29, 2008).

5. John Pettigrew, ed., *Robert Browning, The Poems,* vol. I, 1981, p. 1077.

6. Ibid., p. 1078.

7. Ibid., p. 1092.

Chapter 3. Alfred, Lord Tennyson

1. James D. Kissane, *Alfred Tennyson* (New York: Twayne Publishers, Inc., 1970), p. 21.

2. J. B. Steane, *Tennyson: Literature in Perspective* (London: Evans Brothers Limited, 1966), p. 87.

3. Christopher Ricks, ed., *Tennyson: A Selected Edition* (Berkeley: University of California Press, 1989), p. 138.

Chapter 4. Matthew Arnold

1. "Matthew Arnold," Poetry Foundation, 2008, <http://www.poetryfoundation.org/archive/poet.html?id=222> (April 12, 2008).

2. Matthew Arnold, "From a speech given to the Westminster Teachers' Association on the occasion of his retirement from the office of Inspector," G. W. E. Russell, *Matthew Arnold* (New York: Charles Scribner's Sons, 1904), p. 48; Project Gutenberg, n.d., <http://www.gutenberg.org/files/16745/16745-h/16745-h.htm> (April 12, 2008).

Chapter 5. Christina Rossetti

1. Angela Leighton and Margaret Reynolds, *Victorian Women Poets: An Anthology* (Cambridge, Mass.: Blackwell Publishers, 1995), p. 353.

2. Dolores Rosenblum, *Christina Rossetti: The Poetry of Endurance* (Carbondale and Edwardsville: Southern Illinois University Press, 1986), p. 44.

3. Ibid., p. 46.

Chapter 6. W. B. Yeats

1. R. F. Foster, *W. B. Yeats: A Life. I: The Apprentice Mage 1865–1914* (New York: Oxford University Press, 1997), p. 184.

2. William Butler Yeats, "Nobel Lecture," December 15, 1923, *Nobel Lectures, Literature 1901–1967,* Horst Frenz, ed. (Elsevier Publishing Company, Amsterdam, 1969), The Nobel Foundation, 1923, <http://nobelprize.org/nobel_prizes/literature/laureates/1923/yeats-lecture.html> (April 19, 2008).

Chapter 7. Edith Sitwell

1. Patricia Juliana Smith, "Sitwell, Edith," *glbtq: An Encyclopedia of Gay, Lesbian, Bisexual, Transgender, and Queer Culture,* 2002, <http://www.sitwell.co.uk/literary_sitwells.htm> (April 27, 2008).

2. "The famous literary trio," Renishaw Hall and Gardens, n.d., <http://www.sitwell.co.uk/literary_sitwell.htm> (January 22, 2008).

3. Richard Ellmann and Robert O'Clair, eds., *The Norton Anthology of Modern Poetry,* 2nd edition (New York: W. W. Norton & Company, 1988), p. 448.

4. Joseph Pearce, "Edith Sitwell: Modernity and Tradition," *Lay Witness Magazine,* 2001, <http://www.cuf.org/LayWitness/online_view.asp?lwID=1436> (April 27, 2008).

5. "Edith Sitwell," Poetry Foundation, 2008, <http://www.poetryfoundation.org/archive/poet.html?id=6318> (April 27, 2008).

Chapter 8. Wilfred Owen

1. Paul Fussell, *The Great War and Modern Memory* (New York: Oxford University Press, 1975), p. 81.

2. Wilfred Owen, Letter to Susan Owen, January 16, 1917, *The Wilfred Owen Collection: The First World War Multimedia Digital Archive,* n.d., <http://www.hcu.ox.ac.uk/jtap/images/letters/wo480-1.jpg> (April 27, 2008).

3. Dominic Hibberd, *World War One: Wilfred Owen Audio Gallery,* BBC, n.d., <http://www.bbc.co.uk/history/worldwars/wwone/wilfred_owen_gallery_06.shtml> (April 27, 2008).

4. Fussell, p. 290.

5. Jeremy Paxman, "Wilfred Owen: The Soldiers' Poet," *The Telegraph,* March 11, 2007, <http://www.telegraph.co.uk/arts/main.jhtml?xml=/arts/2007/11/03/boowen103.xml> (April 27, 2008).

Chapter 9. Stevie Smith

1. Anne Bryan, "Strange Attractor," *Stevie Smith Biography,* n.d., <http://www.strange-attractor.co.uk/stevibio.htm> (May 17, 2008).

2. "Stevie Smith," Poetry Foundation, 2008, <http://www.poetryfoundation.org/archive/poet.html?id=6387> (May 17, 2008).

3. Ibid.

4. Stevie Smith on "Not Waving but Drowning," *Poetry Archive,* n.d., <http://www.poetryarchive.org/poetryarchive/singlePoem.do?poemId=7089> (May 17, 2008).

Chapter 10. W. H. Auden

1. Richard Ellmann and Robert O'Clair, eds., *The Norton Anthology of Modern Poetry,* 2nd edition (New York: W. W. Norton & Company, 1988), p. 732.

2. Edward Mendelson, "Preface," *W. H. Auden: Selected Poems,* Edward Mendelson, ed. (New York: Vintage, 1979), p. xiii.

3. Ibid., p. xviii.

4. Claude J. Summers, "Auden, W. H.," *glbtq: An Encyclopedia of Gay, Lesbian, Bisexual, Transgender, and Queer Culture,* 2002, <http://www.glbtq.com/literature/auden_wh.html> (April 20, 2008).

5. Peggy Garland, "Peggy Garland's Memories of Auden," *The W. H. Auden Society Newsletter,* no. 16, May 1997, <http://www.audensociety.org/16newsletter.html#P2_26> (April 20, 2008).

Chapter 11. Dylan Thomas

1. Dylan Thomas, "Reminiscences of Childhood," *Quite Early One Morning* (New York: New Directions, 1968), p. 7; also available on audio at "Dylan Thomas 1914–1953," BBC Four Interviews, n.d., <http://www.bbc.co.uk/bbcfour/audiointerviews/profilepages/thomasd1.shtml> (February 2, 2009).

2. Frank Northen Magill, *Notable Poets: Magill's Choice* (Pasadena, Calif.: Salem Press, 1998), p. 1191.

3. Vernon Watkins, *Dylan Thomas: Letters to Vernon Watkins* (New York: New Directions, 1957), p. 12.

GLOSSARY

allusion—A reference, usually not specific, to a person, place, event, literary text, or artwork.

blank verse—Poetry written in unrhymed iambic pentameter.

couplet—A pair of rhyming lines.

foot—The basic unit of meter in poetry.

iambic pentameter—A rhythm that involves five feet per line of poetry, consisting of an unstressed followed by a stressed syllable.

imagery—Figurative language.

metaphor—A comparison between different things that does not use the words "like" or "as."

meter—The measure of rhythm in poetry, based on the number of syllables within a line and the pattern of stressed and unstressed syllables.

modernism—A twentieth-century artistic and literary movement that broke with tradition to form new modes of expression.

octave—A group of eight lines within a poem.

poet laureate—A well-known and highly respected poet whom the British monarchy appoints to write poems for special events.

Pre-Raphaelite Brotherhood—A group of poets who wished for a return to the techniques and subjects of the Renaissance.

romanticism—A movement in the arts that emphasized emotion, the experience of the common man, and the development of a national folklore.

sextet—A group of six lines within a poem.

simile—A comparison of different things using the words "like" or "as."

sonnet—A poem with fourteen lines, usually in iambic pentameter, with a variety of rhyme patterns.

stanza—A set of lines grouped together within a poem.

symbolism—A movement in poetry and art that began in nineteenth-century France; its main thesis was that objects and images had specific symbolic meanings that could help the artist better portray the spiritual world.

Further Reading

Andronik, Catherine M. *Wildly Romantic: The English Romantic Poets—The Mad, the Bad, and the Dangerous.* New York: Henry Holt and Co., 2007.

Bloom, Harold. *The Best Poems of the English Language: From Chaucer through Frost.* New York: HarperCollins, 2004.

Glancy, Ruth. *Thematic Guide to British Poetry.* Westport, Conn.: Greenwood Press, 2002.

Morris, Jackie. *The Barefoot Book of Classic Poems.* Cambridge, Mass.: Barefoot Books, 2006.

Moses, Brian, ed. *Blood and Roses: British History in Poetry.* London: Hodder Wayland, 2004.

Parisi, Joseph, and Stephen Young, eds. *The Poetry Anthology.* Chicago: Ivan R. Dee, 2004.

Polonsky, Marc. *The Poetry Reader's Toolkit: A Guide to Reading and Understanding Poetry.* Lincolnwood, Ill.: NTC Publishing Group, 1998.

Internet Addresses

Favorite Poem Project
<http://www.favoritepoem.org/>

The Poetry Archive
<http://www.poetryarchive.org/poetryarchive/home.do>

Poetry Foundation
<http://www.poetryfoundation.org>

INDEX

012

NEW HAVEN FREE PUBLIC LIBRARY